the Uprooted

The Collected Papers of Esther Appelberg

Edited by
Harriet A. Feiner

Child Welfare League of America

Library of Congress Catalog Card Number: 77-85136
ISBN: 0-87868-169-8

Acknowledgments

Respect, admiration, friendship and a deep sense of loss brought the members of The Esther Appelberg Memorial Committee together. Students, colleagues and friends, we searched for an appropriate way to honor Dr. Appelberg's memory and to express the individual feelings we had for her. It soon became clear that a volume of her own writings would be the most fitting memorial. Social work colleagues and future students could then continue to utilize the legacy of her original and creative thinking.

Organizing a project like this is a difficult task and could not have been accomplished without the dedication, cooperation and concerted effort of many people. On behalf of The Esther Appelberg Memorial Committee, I wish to thank all of those who contributed the money, time and energy that made this volume possible. As chairman of the committee and editor of the volume, I wish to extend my thanks to my fellow committee members who helped the work to proceed so smoothly. Although all of those who helped are too numerous to mention, the editorial assistance of Deborah Miller, Alan Bernstein and Naomi Abramowitz was invaluable. Special thanks must also go to Carl Schoenberg of the Child Welfare League of America, who understood the value of this undertaking and facilitated publication by the League. His knowledge and expertise were essential in the preparation of this volume.

Harriet A. Feiner

iii

FOR ESTHER

Like the mysterious arch
Her will, stressed and tortured,
Strengthens in response.

In an arid soil of fortune
A tropical flowering of
Love and discipline has firmly rooted
Soul-nourishing.

She is a generous spirit,
Who when presented with
Friendship's bill
Never asked how much it cost.

David Bernstein

This poem was written immediately after the news of Esther Appelberg's heart attack. It was enjoyed with her, not knowing then that she would die 2 days later.

A Tribute

It is a privilege to join this enterprise honoring Esther Appelberg but it is no pleasure. Besides all else, she had a talent for friendship and we miss her. It were better to be contributing to a *Festschrift* than to this volume of her collected papers published posthumously. One marveled always at the many persons from various life paths who counted among her friends and associates. Age and position had no role in the continuing and meaningful relationships she inspired. What manner of person left such loyalties in her wake?

In her life and in her spirit, Esther Appelberg symbolized our generation's saddest events, which, at the same time, instigated some of the greatest responses of which man is capable. Out of the Nazi holocaust she emerged successively as victim, then witness, and eventually as redeemer for man's inhumanity to his fellow. All of us are witnesses, albeit mostly silent; nearly all of us are victims. But it takes nobility to rebound from being victim to redeemer, and this is especially so when reparation is offered for damage one has oneself only witnessed but not wrought. To give because of compassion rather than guilt is social work at its finest. She and those like her offer the model that the rest of us fail.

The sufferings of Esther Appelberg and her relatives left a depressive scar on her personality, a sadness familiar in many Jews of her experience. But she did not treasure hurt as a permanent justification for later weakness. Rather, she put her high intelligence and her shrewd energy to tasks of helping and training others to help, for she was also a superb teacher. This book is evidence of her gift as an engaged witness.

Esther Appelberg was born in 1923 in Hamburg, where she completed eight grades of schooling. She entered the Jewish Children's Center for training, which also prepared young people for emigration to Palestine. In 1939 she went to Palestine, attended the Mizrahi Teachers College for Women in Jerusalem, and just before graduation in 1944, was sent to set up a new school in a small collective village. These experiences were decisive in determining the direction of her professional life; it was the educational and social problems of children rather than teaching that evolved as her main interest.

She returned to Jerusalem a year later to work in a youth trade union, carrying responsibility for adolescents in offices, shops, factories and laboratories, safeguarding their rights as workers and helping them plan further educational and vocational studies in evening classes. She was only 24 when the Jewish Agency for Palestine sent her to Germany to serve in a subunit to the United Nations Relief and Rehabilitation Administration and the International Relief Organization, as welfare and education officer in displaced persons camps and Jewish communities. Later, when the State of Israel was established, she served as transport officer escorting groups of displaced persons from Munich to Marseilles en route to Israel.

In 1949 she was back in Jerusalem to set up a visiting teacher program for truants and children with emotional and study problems, and this brought her in close cooperation with a child guidance clinic. A scholarship awarded by the National Council of Jewish Women of America in 1951 made it possible for her to attend the School of Applied Social Sciences at Western Reserve University, earn an M.S. degree, and expand her interest in foster home and adoption settings. Once more returned to Jerusalem in 1953, she became district supervisor in a public child welfare agency. To quote her own report, "This work confronted me with some of the most basic dilemmas in Israel (at the time), such as the gap between old-timer and newcomer, the insecurity of the uprooted immigrant and the intrafamilial tensions created through transplantation to a new culture. . . . I think that the knowledge and experience of 1½ years in the Ministry of Welfare constituted the major contribution to my ability to perform other jobs, such as work with disturbed children and parents in a clinical setting, counseling youth leaders and housemothers in institutions and collective settlements (kibbutzim) and teaching principles and methods of social work in the Tel Aviv and Jerusalem schools of social work." Only under such pressures and with full engagement are social work's experts formed while still relatively young!

Wanting to strengthen her knowledge of dynamic theory and treatment technique, Dr. Appelberg next worked as a psychiatric social worker at the Lasker Mental Hygiene Clinic with disturbed children and parents. Simultaneously, she developed a training program for youth leaders, counselors, housemothers and teachers in agricultural children's villages and collective settlements, helping them deal with cultural conflicts, shifts in values, deprivations, and adjustment problems in a new country. When Youth Aliyah set up a child guidance clinic, Dr. Appelberg helped in its formation. She became Senior Psychiatric Social Worker, supervising, participating in policy formulation, and initiating new projects involving parents and educators in behalf of the children.

Concurrently with her other work, Dr. Appelberg supervised students for the School of Social Work of the Tel Aviv municipality, and in 1953 taught courses in casework and child welfare at that school. Later she taught also at the School of Social Work in Jerusalem.* These 4 years of teaching, she wrote, "enabled me to conceptualize social work theory, help students integrate theory and practice, systematically build up a case record library and compile a bibliography." Active in professional affairs, she was vice chairman of the Israel Association of Graduate and Social Casework and subsequently its chairman. It was these activities that prompted her return to Case Western Reserve University in 1956 for doctoral studies and a teaching career.

To support these advanced studies, she worked full time as a cottage unit supervisor at the Bellefaire Regional Treatment Center for emotionally disturbed children. I was teaching at the School of Applied Social Sciences at the time, and was soon to begin a program of research at Bellefaire focused on verbal accessibility, a concept involved in Dr. Appelberg's dissertation. Looking back, it is impressive that nothing about her manner in moving about the campus of the institution or talking with the children suggested the status she had had

---

* At the time two separate schools of social work existed, one in Jerusalem under the Ministry of Welfare and the second in Tel Aviv sponsored by the municipality of Tel Aviv. The Paul Baerwald School of Social Work of the Hebrew University in Jerusalem, which opened in 1958, was an outgrowth of these two schools. In 1969 the Tel Aviv School of Social Work of Tel Aviv University was established.

in Israel. She was simple in her directness and as focused on each child as if this were the only case she was carrying. I can even recall her giving my own clinical notions a hearing of greater apparent respectfulness than, at that time, they surely deserved, for she was nothing if not tactful. She had the kind of dignity and lack of pretense accessible only to those who are quite other-engaged. In a much later episode, she accompanied her uncle, the great Hebrew writer S. Y. Agnon, to the ceremonies in Stockholm at which he became a Nobel Laureate. Her reports of this adventure, too, contained no hint of self-importance.

After achieving the D.S.W. in 1961, Dr. Appelberg settled in the United States, joined the faculty of the Wurzweiler School of Social Work at Yeshiva University, and taught there until her death in 1975. Although still young for death, she had lived in and adapted to three cultures, and had held a surprising variety of positions. The two enduring, evidently uninterruptible, themes in her existence were the desire to find ever more effective ways to help those whose lives were marked by disruption, separation and loss, and the impulsion to subject her many and varied experiences to ordering by her considerable intellect.

Her perceptiveness informs the papers assembled here. Each summarizes an aspect of an experience in which she had been immersed at the time. An early one is a paper on supervision published in Israel when she was 29; the last one deals with record keeping and the rights of children. Between these are major papers on child welfare, work with families, the psychology of displaced persons and other professional themes.

The organizing principle of this book is to be found in the life course and service of its author. Social workers and others concerned with child welfare, with learning and teaching, and with the multitude of displaced persons in our time will all be richly rewarded by these pages.

How shall I end? Surely, Dr. Appelberg would disapprove strongly were I to act as intellectual pallbearer. She, too, was a survivor, so I recall her loneliness and our own missed opportunities to have been more helpful to her. Perhaps she would be best pleased with this tribute: here was a truly expert witness. Shalom!

Norman A. Polansky
School of Social Work
University of Pennsylvania

Contents

Child Welfare

Introduction

Written between 1962 and 1974, this series of articles on child welfare reflects an intense dedication to finding better ways of providing for children whose lives are disrupted by separation and loss. Dr. Appelberg's sensitive concern, sharp intelligence, and capacity to think in new directions enabled her to develop important new approaches.

Her ideas grew out of her deep understanding of human growth and development, as well as her respect for the sanctity of life and the rights that this sanctity implies. Her interest was in how needs can be met, rather than in how things were traditionally done. Consequently, she gave serious attention to the feelings of children who were the unavoidable victims of the inevitably changing worker. In "The Dependent Child and the Changing Worker" she made suggestions for procedures that might alleviate some of the trauma related to change.

In "Children in Limbo," she expressed some of her ideas on new approaches to foster care. Along with other suggestions, she highlighted the necessity of using time limits constructively so that we do not continue to create more "children in limbo."

In "The Case Against Records," written during her last springtime, she raised questions about the entire tradition of record keeping, par-

3

ticularly in view of social work's concern with the right to privacy and confidentiality.

Each article demonstrates Dr. Appelberg's interest in those small aspects of daily life that together profoundly affect the quality of life, as well as the ways in which children grow. Her insights remain as pertinent and important today as when she put them to paper.

Harriet A. Feiner

Children in Limbo - Foster Care and Nowhere to Go

This paper is concerned only with children who are about to enter placement, and offers some suggestions on what we can do so they will not become "children in limbo." Basic to this are several assumptions: 1) The sheer number of children already in placement makes it impossible to undo all of what has been done. We may have to look at those already in placement as the "generation of the desert," like their biblical counterparts, the Jews who wandered in the desert but never reached their destination, the Holy Land. 2) There will always be children who will have to live away from their biological parents, and the task, therefore, is to help these children not to become another "generation of the desert." 3) We must learn to use ourselves and our facilities differently.

Each one of us can tell about successes as well as failures in placement. Yet we know little about the number of successes, the number of failures, or why we succeed with some children and fail with others. The definition of "need" is highly complex.[1] The problems that precipitated placement for children already in foster care are not necessarily the same as those that precipitate placement today or that will precipitate placement in the future. A significant study of "true need" in relation to child placement is difficult to carry out, since accurate measurement of inadequate parental functioning is hard if not impossible. Nevertheless the concept of demand, with recognition that this may be an underestimation of true need, is probably a good estimate, since the problems precipitating placement are usually the result of urgent situations that have high visibility and represent issues that are of great concern to the general community.[2]

Although factors associated with placement have fluctuated and changed, and will continue to fluctuate due to the changing character of society, economics and community resources, certain problems have always been with us and will continue to be in the future—out-of-wedlock children, psychosocial and economic stresses, children's behavior problems, parental incapacity, and child abuse. The definition of these problems is obviously influenced by geography, race, ethnicity, economics, community attitudes and resources, and professional and nonprofessional judgment; for example, changing attitudes toward out-of-wedlock children have already caused some shift in placement requests. The number of children in placement has continued to increase over the years. The implication is that planning for children's services will have to continue on several levels: 1) changes in law; 2) provision of more and better services for children in their own homes, such as day care centers, special services in schools, homemaker services, financial assistance, counseling, and other kinds of help; 3) provision of more and better services for children entering placement, as well as for those already in placement; 4) the development of better educated personnel.

Psychological Needs

A study of requests for foster care in seven metropolitan areas [3] indicated that though economically disadvantaged families were heavily represented in its sample, the overwhelming majority of the children were white and from economically independent families. The nonwhites were probably underrepresented, reflecting more limited availability of services to them. With more and better services available, the number of children requiring placement might well rise. Often, only as people have adequate economic conditions do they experience and become conscious of their psychological problems. It is hard to think about emotional needs when overwhelmed by the demands of an empty stomach. As basic concrete needs are met, increased incidence of psychosocial stress frequently occurs. Although action is not only needed but long overdue, it is also evident that good results are dependent upon the provision of services for the human psyche along with concrete services and community action. That man does not live by bread alone is demonstrated by the increasing evidence of emotional stress and isolation in our society. Sharply increasing divorce rates, problems of drug abuse, rising demands for psychological services even in community action programs, all highlight the importance of providing better psychological services even as we work for the resolution of the race problem. This implies more, not less, knowledge about what makes the human being tick. Falling short of this approach risks the danger of further dehumanization of services—programs or actions that lack soul. The belief that economic and racial equality will eliminate psychic problems fails to recognize that every solution of a problem carries within it the creation of a new problem; since a solution is a compromise of conflicting pulls, ignored desires or needs will continue to demand satisfaction. Problem solving is a continuous process. I often doubt that economic problems have a final cure, but I have no doubt whatsoever that psychic problems have no total cure. People must live with their scars, and, it is hoped, learn to live differently and to some extent better in the future.

Out of all that we know about children in placement, I emphasize only those factors that seem most crucial: intake, the decision for placement, preplacement and the first year of placement. Within this framework, I address the biological parent, the foster parent, the child, the community and the agency.

Intake

At point of intake it must be decided whether this is short-term or long-term placement, whether the parents will retain guardianship or will give it up to the agency or foster parent, or whether they will free the child altogether and surrender him for adoption. This is not a one-time decision, but a dynamic process that, within a time limit, leads to and allows for shifts toward the final decision. However, it is only when we are clear about the obligation to arrive at a decision with the parents that we can plan for the child and make sure that children entering placement do not become children in limbo because of the lack of a clear plan. It is during the first year of placement that biological parents tend to disappear or to become available for contact with the agency only infrequently and on an arbitrary basis. Lack of clarity, lack of decision, lack of contact between agency and parent, often contribute to their disappearance.

Preplacement

Parental participation in planning for the child is a "must." Although professionals agree on this point, one wonders to what degree participation in planning by both parents is carried out.

The study cited previously reports: "In an overwhelming majority of instances the child's mother reportedly knew of the placement plan. Usually they agreed with it and cooperated in carrying it out. For only 5% of the children were the mothers reported *not* to have known of the plan; 10% *not* to have agreed; and 14% *not* to have cooperated. Lack of participation of the mother in planning was true principally in the deviant parent behavior group and to a lesser extent in the psychological stress group. Fathers were much less likely to be informed of and involved in planning than mothers, but the incompleteness of the data on their participation makes the specific figures of dubious import." [4,5]

There will always be children whose parents will not know, will not agree, or will not cooperate. The statistics may not reflect the situation as it actually is. Assuming that the judgment of the individual worker varies as to what is involved in knowledge, agreement and cooperation, one might arrive at a lower number for the real agreement and a cooperation, not only of mothers, but especially of fathers. After all, fathers are the forgotten men in social work. Although some recent literature reflects recognition of the father's influence, practice is still poor. Knowledge about parental resistance to involvement in after-care [5] is another indication that the number of biological parents who are in real agreement with plans and who cooperate before and during placement is even lower than we think.

The return of the child to his biological parents is another highly critical factor in the whole process. The resistance of parents to professional help for themselves and their children at this crucial point would be lower if the parents had been real and consistent partners all along. It is too late to start working with parents when we decide to return a child to them. Note that I say "we return." Not only does the parent resent not having had a say in this decision, but frequently he has made his adjustment to separation from the child.

True clinical awareness of the importance of aftercare has increased lately, yet practice has not kept up with this awareness. A highly skilled worker who has a sound base of psychological understanding will be better able to involve actively resistant parents than a worker who lacks these qualities or lacks conviction about parents' active involvement in placement.

If we agree that parental knowledge and agreement to placement are not enough, we must carry out the principle of active participation of both parents and define this principle more sharply. Furthermore, since members of the parental population vary in their capacities, one measure of parental participation cannot be applied to all parents indiscriminately. More and different approaches to increasing parental participation during this first crucial year are required.

Individualizing Treatment

In theory we know that each individual is unique and treatment should be geared to this uniqueness. Yet in practice, too often we have failed to individualize treatment. Perhaps in no other field of social work have we so clearly failed to live up to professed values as in work with parents whose children need placement away from home. We have recognized that different children need different kinds of placement and that parents differ about the kinds of placement they will allow for their children. We have defined categories of reasons for placement that in themselves should have been indicators for different treatment of parents. We have talked about parents as partners and about the importance of their retention of parental obligations and rights. Yet most of the time we have not gone beyond two measures of participation for all of them. Across the board we have asked for money and visiting—albeit even visiting has often been restricted by the agency. Although both measures are important, they have often been applied in a one-sided way, frequently without consideration of the differing motivations and capacities for parental participation. Consequently, the level of parental responsibility, set mainly by the agency, has often been insufficient to sustain parental interest and permit active involvement in and concern for the child's life. Agency decisions have reflected attention to the pathology and weakness of the parents, rather than to their health and strength.

In short, though we may have to be satisfied for some parents only to know about and agree to placement, others could and should be involved in the preplacement visit. They can be the ones to tell the prospective foster parent about the child's likes and dislikes, about what he eats and what he takes to bed with him. Others can take their children for medical checkups, or can enroll them in the new school, sign the report card, confer with the teacher, or take the child for an overnight or even longer visit. Some could probably spend holidays with the foster parents if the latter are willing. Often agencies have been too restrictive in scheduling contacts between foster and biological parents. These examples are not listed in order of importance, but should be looked at according to more sharply defined diagnostic criteria. Capacities of parents, the nature of the disturbances of the child, and the plan for reunion must all be considered. The process must be a dynamic one that accounts for change and growth. A parent might begin by holding on to only one or two of these parental rights and obligations. Later, when the child is already in placement, the parent might be able to take on additional responsibilities. It is needless to stress that the parental role will influence agency work with foster parents and their roles.

A newer experimental approach might be the possibility of placing parent and child together in a suitable arrangement, with all possible variations of only day or night placement, or full-time care.

Foster Parents

To open one's home to a stranger—especially to a child who, more often than not and for whatever reasons, has been deprived emotionally or economically, who is, even with the best preparation, in a state of confusion, and mourning the loss of parents—demands great sensitivity, flexibility, alertness and ability to give of oneself. It involves a shift in the foster parents' family relationships, a disturbance in their equilibrium, and the need to establish a new balance. This means that there will be a different kind of relationship between the foster parents and their own children. If placement is to be successful, the foster child has to be included in this new Gestalt. This is by no means an easy task for the foster parents, particularly because few anticipate it. Recognizing foster parents' crucial task in the first year, we have to address these aspects so that frequent replacement or pressures to take in an additional child they really do not want can be avoided.

Inherent in all of the foregoing are criteria for work with foster parents and for work with the child and the community. Some changes have taken place in our professional attitudes, as well as in what we look for in foster parents.[7] To an extent this has expressed itself in practice in the acceptance of widows and public assistance clients as foster parents. However, we still continue, though we profess differently, to look for housing instead of looking for people who could be foster parents and open their houses, which might then be homes. If we look for people instead of housing, if we carefully assess the situation of the child and the parents so that we can know what the capacities of the biological parents are—whether the parents will remain involved, whether the child will return to his parents, whether the child will remain in placement for years to come, or whether the child will be released for adoption—then we shall be better able to understand and differentiate the kinds of foster parent we need for different circumstances and situations. Parents who have the capacity to hold onto and develop their parental roles need foster parents who can tolerate this kind of partnership with parents, in addition to their partnership with agency personnel.

Foster parents willing and able to enter into such partnerships with biological parents will be those who have considerable ego strength, great tolerance for deviation, conviction about the importance of biological parents to the child, and satisfaction with their own children. Just as we are now more often open to single-parent adoption, we might look for those qualities in single women or widows. Foster parents—couples or single women—may be found who can use day care for children of all ages, either because they work or because day care centers make available opportunities for the development of the child. We have to look for and help those who are willing to make a career of foster parenthood. This might mean a greater development and reliance ·on group homes and small residences run by single women and men.

Foster parents who are willing to share parental responsibilities with biological parents might also be those from whom we can select big sisters or brothers for new or less knowledgeable foster parents, and who can be actively involved in agency programs of foster parent education.

If we look for this kind of foster parent we might be more able to attract additional groups of persons who are willing to open their homes. In addition, we shall have to invest more professional manpower in the education rather than the training of foster parents, so they can function more independently, find their own answers, and know when to consult the expert. Training, in contrast to education, is task oriented, narrower and more limited in its results. In the end it is more expensive, less satisfying and less fruitful, as it seldom leads to autonomy. For those children who are in effect without parents, either because they have been abandoned or because their parents have an extreme degree of pathology, we can be less concerned with the ability of foster parents to permit biological parents to be their partners.

Guardianship

Differentiation of foster parents for different foster children also requires a new look at the concept of guardianship.[8, 9] Some foster parents can function also as guardians for foster children whose parents cannot be guardians. Those who are able to function independently after a preparatory period might be given this important responsibility. This would free agency personnel to devote greater time to biological parents and to those foster parents who do need attention. Foster parents who assume legal guardianship might well play a role similar to adoptive parents in a subsidized adoption. Intensive help should be provided during the first year of placement. Since both foster parents and child will have experienced a positive helping relationship, they should feel free to come back to the agency or other community resources should the need arise. Preparation for the possibility of future need for counseling at critical developmental stages would be part of our work during the crucial probationary period.

Foster parents have been and are active in parent-teacher groups for their own children, but we have neglected to help them become involved in parent-teacher groups in the schools of their foster children. Yet we know that many children in placement have learning problems. Their teachers and the parents of other children are not aware of what it means to be a foster child, and often treat them with prejudice.

Increased board rates for all foster parents, plus fringe benefits such as sick leave and vacations, will have to be established to increase the pool of persons willing to become foster parents. State and federal money will have to play a greater role than it has played so far. A tax deduction for foster children might be a step toward a more attractive board rate. Nonetheless, we shall probably always have to count on motivation that does not depend primarily on remuneration in dollars and cents.

Professional workers have frequently failed to appreciate the lobbying functions some foster parents are equipped and ready to perform. When foster parents group together, they may see themselves as adversaries of agencies and workers rather than as advocates for children, but with agency sanction and help, they can become a pressure group for child welfare legislation and programs. We might then get some of the money needed for better programs. Who is better able than the foster parent to talk to the legislator and to the community about the plight of the child in limbo? Who is better able to share with other foster parents the knowledge and experience about how to bring up somebody else's children and how to get along with their parents, than many of the experienced foster parents?

Categories of Placed Child

Placed children fall into three general groupings: 1) children whose parent or parents remain in the picture to a varying degree all through placement; 2) children born out of wedlock whose mothers relinquish them; 3) children whose parents disappear and then re-appear to retain and claim parental rights.

I do not know what is worse for a child—to be a living orphan or to be a real orphan; [10] to be born out of wedlock and not know where one comes from, or to know one's name and where one comes from, yet at the same time to experience one's parents as totally unde-pendable, vague figures who sometimes appear from nowhere for an hour or a day, perhaps with presents fit for a king or perhaps in an alcoholic rage, and then vanish as suddenly into thin air. I do know that every child in placement needs help to cope with the trauma of separation, with his fantasies about and rage toward his parents, with his conflicts of loyalty to parents and foster parents, and with his questions about his identity. The degree, the frequency, the depth of help depend on the age of the child, the nature of his problem, the reason for placement, the circumstances in the foster home, the avail-ability of significant persons in his life other than foster parents, such as older siblings or other blood relatives. It is fair neither to the child nor to the foster parents to leave it to the foster parents to help the child come to terms with these problems. We cannot ask foster parents to carry the responsibility for discussing major areas of emotional conflict with the child. This is the responsibility of a skilled profes-sional helper.

The Question of Name

We also have to rethink some old beliefs. One is that the child has to continue to carry his biological name. [11] Social workers have a strong belief in the importance of parents, and in the fifth command-ment, "Thou shall honor thy parents." However, most of us come from parents who loved us and fulfilled their parental obligations. [12] It is hard for us to imagine that some parents treat their children badly. Giving up one's parents' name is to us a rejection of our parents, of part of ourselves, a loss of identity. Yet what identity can be at-tached to a name that has no face, that carries with it an experience of rejection, of not being cared for or loved? If the child has to be in long-term foster care until he comes of age, if his foster parents will be the ones who give him the feeling of being wanted and cared for, would it not sometimes be better that he be called by their name? Have we ever considered what it means to be Joe Smith at school and to tell teacher and classmates that we live with the Browns? By being Joe Smith and living with the Browns, Joe is set apart from his classmates. He is looked at as different and is never allowed to forget it. In our society being different means that something is wrong with us. Would it not be enough if foster parents and foster child knew Joe's original name? Each of us has some family secret, a skeleton in the closet. A family name is not enough to give identity.

We have to define more clearly what children need and for how long a time: casework, group work, psychiatric help, tutoring, health care or some combination of services. Implicit is the concept of help as a process that allows for shifts and changes. Not all children who spend years in placement need a social worker the entire time. There comes a point of diminishing returns. We have to be less ambitious and more realistic. We all know children who have been "over-social-worked," and who talk the lingo with such ease that they put to shame many a professional, especially the beginner. They are the hardest to reach; their talk is not connected with feelings; their capacity for relationship is poor; their trust in the worker is slight; they have seen too many come and go.[13] Some of these are the children who talk about "my agency." The only comfort we can take is that they relate at least to the agency or the institution that cared for them. At least they know where to go if they need help.

The Child and His Siblings

We have often failed to help the placed child retain or form meaningful relations with those siblings who remained at home or who are also in foster care. How often have we decided on separate placements for siblings! We think, because of sibling rivalry, or severe parental deprivation, each child now needs someone who will take care only of him. Yet, these children have to compete with the foster parents' own children. We have looked only at the negative in the situation instead of at the potential positive, and thereby have not helped brothers and sisters to retain or form reasonably good and meaningful relationships with each other. For children who grow up without parents to depend upon, such relationships are extremely important if the children are to combat present and future loneliness and preserve or plan resources for family life.

The Community

The child who goes into placement usually moves into a new neighborhood. Frequently this new neighborhood represents a higher socioeconomic status, different mores and values. It does not tolerate deviant behavior. The school requires more than most foster children can deliver, especially at the point of placement. The foster child is frequently an underachiever who daydreams, lacks concentration and motivation to get ahead. All of this puts him into conflict with his foster parents and their schools. The school and other community resources are poorly equipped to understand and empathize with foster children or to help them. Many of the negative attitudes in the neighborhood come from lack of knowledge, fear and racial prejudice. We have failed to help the community to integrate foster parents and the foster child. How many replacements, especially in the crucial first year, can be attributed to this failure? At best, these attitudes have hindered the foster child from benefiting fully from what the new neighborhood has to offer him.

The Agency

The agency and its worker have to be clear and convinced about the importance of this crucial early period in the placement process. Only then will they see to it that a plan is developed and followed through. Whenever agencies or caseworkers are asked what is needed for the child already in foster care, we hear demands for more facilities, such as homes, clinics, staff, as well as resources in the community, so that placement can be prevented. Seldom do we hear that we have to use ourselves differently. It seems to me that we are caught in a kind of circular thinking because of the tremendous pressures in child placement. The shortage of manpower does not allow the worker to sit back and take stock of himself, his work, and the problems he faces. He often does not see interrelationships, or how wrong beginnings and certain deficits create a chain reaction of other deficits resulting in more and different problems. If we do not learn how to use ourselves and our foster parents differently, we shall continue to go in circles. Facilities need a soul. It is through the relationship, a vital ingredient in the social process, that we can help the client to use the facilities so that he can have a better life.

In conclusion, I have implied some difference in the concept of placement—that placement per se be considered a temporary measure in response to a crisis. In itself it is never a solution. Placement has to be considered a temporary treatment plan, to be used dynamically by the caseworker to decide with the parent and the child: whether the child will return home; whether he will go into long-term foster care with parent, relative, friend of family, foster parent, agency or state appointed as guardian; or whether the child will be surrendered for adoption. Parents have strengths as well as weaknesses—pathology as well as health. We have to address ourselves to both areas. Instead of working for or on behalf of parents, we must work with the parents, mother and father, all the way through. Nevertheless, the work must take place with full recognition of the pressure of the passage of time and the possible consequence—inadequate emotional development of the child. If the interests of the child and his well-being are endangered, we must make a decision in behalf of and in favor of the child. Children who have been abused or whose parents do not fulfill parental responsibilities must be protected. We must remember that children are not chattel and parents do not own them. If parents cannot or do not make and carry out a plan for them, we shall have to go to court so that they can be free. In these cases the child and only the child is our client; we must be truly in loco parentis. It may appear to be a choice between two evils, but at least it will be the lesser one, to the best of our knowledge and conscience. Inaction also is a choice and has consequences. We have done well with many children, but we can do better for many more. Since each child is a world, each child we save is a world saved.

Notes and References

1. The Need for Foster Care, An Incidence Study of Requests for Foster Care and Agency Response in Seven Metropolitan Areas. New York: Child Welfare League of America, 1969, p. 1.
2. Ibid., p. 2.
3. Ibid., p. 3.
4. Ibid., pp. 43-45.
5. Helen D. Stone. Reflections on Foster Care. Child Welfare League of America, 1969, p. 29.
6. Ibid., pp. 24-28.
7. Ibid., pp. 27-28.
8. Esther Appelberg. "The Significance of Personal Guardianship for Children in Casework," Child Welfare, XLIX, 1, 1970. Also, Source Book of Teaching Materials on Welfare of Children, Council on Social Work Education, New York, 1969.
9. Ibid., p. 34.
10. Stone points out that workers do not see actual abandonment of children by parents as a major problem. Although I acknowledge the difference between legal abandonment and emotional abandonment, I wonder whether the child acknowledges these differences and can live with them. Is the feeling of abandonment really perceived in all its harshness by the worker? It seems to me that Stone has the same impression as I have. Op. cit., p. 34.
11. Some agencies are experimenting in this area.
12. Our attitude toward parents, as expressed in work with them, is highly ambivalent and contradictory.
13. Esther Appelberg. "The Dependent Child and the Changing Worker," Child Welfare, XLVIII, 7, July 1969.

The Dependent Child and the Changing Worker

Since innumerable books and articles have been written about the trauma of separation in general, and its effects on children specifically, it is curious that so little casework literature is addressed to the theoretical and practical implications of reassigning clients from one worker to another. Sidney Z. and Miriam S. Moss have pointed to the lack of writing dealing specifically with this question.[1] A survey of the literature discloses few papers dealing with the impact on the client of the worker's leaving.[2] As early as 1947, Regina Flesch, disturbed by "the transiency of professional personnel," raised the question·"as to the wisdom of embarking upon any important treatment interviews of a long-term nature without some guarantee as to the stability of the relationship. If we are dubious about how long we may be at the service of the client, perhaps we should be more discriminating about developing more relationships that later must be broken, with severe disturbances to the client. The client may well ask what business we have in engaging in relationship therapy if we do not expect to continue either relationship or therapy."[3]

Clients say, "I know agencies; they always change the person you see. There is never just one. They don't stay with you." The client is telling us, "I don't want to start because I don't want to part." Typical

---

Published originally in Child Welfare, XLVIII, 7, July 1969.

of the cynicism the client develops is the remark of -a 16-year-old girl in foster home placement, at the time of her first interview with me: "You are my eighth caseworker in 6 years. What do you want me to tell you?"

For the child in placement, the situation is further complicated, since he has already undergone the trauma of separation from his family. Separation is especially traumatic for children who have had parents unable to establish stable bonds with them. A second experience of premature separation from a significant person is likely to weaken the ability of the child to relate to .other human beings, and in some instances such a child loses entirely the capacity to relate in a positive way.[4] The reference, of course, is not to normal individuation. Normal individuation comes about through the process of separation,[5] beginning about the age of 6 months when the infant first distinguishes between self and nonself, and continuing, for example, as the toddler can let his mother leave on an errand, or the child can separate from his mother to go to nursery school. The concern here is with separation resulting from the loss of significant persons in the child's life.

Use of Transference

The casework relationship contains transference elements. Positive transference can be an ally in working with a client. The use of transference in work with children, however—especially with children who live with their parents—is more complicated because the child's libido is still directed to them.[6] In institution treatment, the situation becomes further complicated because of multiple transference.[7] "It is known that at the time of termination and especially at termination due to the worker's leaving, our greatest ally can become the most difficult obstacle in reassignment of clients. It is impossible to pick up the relationship and give it bodily to the new worker, along with the client, and it is usually equally impossible to work through all the transference problems before reassigning the case."[8]

It is recognized that there are clients, and among them children, who can overcome this obstacle and form new relationships. It is also recognized that for some children, transference exists toward institutions, such as church, hospital, or treatment institutions. All who work with children in placement know the child who returns year after year to visit the institution, even ·though the worker who once worked with him has left. Similar are the children who do not talk about caseworkers, but about agencies. We also know clients who start to progress only when they do get a new worker, and clients whose diagnostically planned termination makes for speedier recovery and self-reliance. Nonetheless, many children, especially those in placement, have been severely traumatized by frequent changes in caseworkers and other child care personnel.

Participation in Planning

In their discussion, the Mosses [9] point to the "value of the client's having some control over the ending process; he should be able to participate in the decision to terminate treatment . . ." In practice, the importance of this matter of control is generally recognized in work with adult clients, but tends to be overlooked in work with children. The child usually does not enter placement out of recognition of a need for help. Other persons—parents, parent surrogates, teachers —send him for care or treatment. He may be placed because his parents, due to their own problems, cannot care for him; or because placement is the treatment recommended for his own problems. Whatever the reasons, once it is decided that a child is to be placed, he needs help to understand the reason, and to work through the trauma of separation.

A change in workers presents a child with a situation similar to that at the time of placement. He has little control over ending with his accustomed worker or beginning with a new one. In child guidance clinics, parents who have not overcome their resistance to treatment may use a change of workers as a rationale for ending, and remove the child from the clinic. In such a situation, intensified work with the parents is required to prevent a premature ending of treatment. It is different in a placement situation, where the parents have no control over whether the child should continue with another worker. Sometimes parents are not consulted at all. Such practice is questionable. If parents are encouraged to have a part in the treatment of their child, the process involved in changing workers can offer an opportunity for enlisting the active support of the parents. The whole experience may result in therapeutic gain for both parents and child.

Verbal Accessibility

It is not known under what conditions or for how long a change in workers may retard the client. Experience indicates that the change is likely to lower a client's verbal accessibility for a time. Verbal accessibility has been defined as the ability to discuss painful feelings with others. This ability apparently does not vary with the length of stay in an institution. Also, it has been found "that a person's verbal accessibility is a stable characteristic of the personality, that fluctuates only within certain limits." [10]

It was found that an adolescent who was open, was open to everyone. The degree of openness varied, but within certain limits. Although verbal accessibility is not the same as treatability, it is important in casework, and it may be hypothesized that a child verbally accessible to one caseworker will be accessible to another. Yet it may be assumed that the verbally accessible adolescent will not be so ready to communicate painful feelings to a new person as to a trusted, significant person in his life. It is not known when he will again become accessible, how deep his regression will be, how damaging the trauma, how strong his resistance, but it can be assumed that these will depend not only on the individual life history, but on the nature of transference and how effectively the outgoing caseworker has prepared the child for a new worker. Clinical experience confirms that children do, of course, "survive." Some children, after initial regression, quickly establish a relation with the new worker. But frequent changes retard treatment in many children, creating and reactivating trauma, and prolonging sickness. This in turn increases the costs of care and treatment.

Handling a Change in Workers

The Mosses pointed out: "On the basis of recent figures on turnover, one in four caseworkers who were on the job at the beginning of the 1967 may be expected to leave before the end of the year." [11]

Considering the widening opportunities and ever-increasing demand for social work manpower, the caseworker's mobility may now be even greater than one in four. When we consider the rapid turnover of other child care personnel such as foster parents and counselors and other personnel in institutions, the number of changes in caseworker and in other significant individuals that a placed child is likely to undergo becomes overwhelming. This situation demands a hard look at social work practice, and a search for ways of changing it.

There is little literature about how a change in worker is handled. In practice, it appears that, once a child has begun with a new worker, contact with the previous worker has to be ended. Continuation of contact with a former worker is considered to be detrimental and likely to interfere with the child's forming a relationship with his new worker. The same is held true when the child goes from one foster parent to another, from one institution to another, or from foster care into adoption. This approach seems to disregard psychodynamic knowledge about the impact of separation. The writer has had experience in continuing contact (through letters and presents) with a number of children who were transferred to other agencies and to new workers in a new setting. The practice was based on this theory: A person experiences loss in a change of workers, but even if he is a sick child or adolescent, he can form more than one relationship. Not cutting off contact completely can diminish feelings of loss and pain, and avoid feelings of worthlessness. Since the worker does not totally disappear, the child can better accept the reason for the separation from the worker, rather than experience it only as rejection and desertion. It is the responsibility of the former worker not to interfere with the new treatment relationship; it is the responsibility of the new worker to use the child's relation to the former worker in a positive way. This way of working was effective with war orphans of World War II, Nazi victims such as infants or toddlers who had lost their parents.

Children, even the most severely disturbed, know how to use adults in different capacities, and are usually well aware of the differences in role and function of adults.[12] Any who have difficulty making this differentiation should be helped. The more progress children make in their treatment, the more they are able to form relationships outside the treatment situation, and, as a result, the less need they have to address themselves to a former worker. The writer's experience has borne this out; the time came when the children felt no need, or little need, to hear from the former worker. When a client was reassured that, despite the change, the former worker could still be contacted, the need for contact vanished; [13] the knowledge of possible support was enough. In this way, a child's experience with a former worker can serve as a model for other relationships. The child learns that his need for a particular person gradually lessens. As he becomes ready to separate, parting can be a positive experience.

Although many social workers still do not favor allowing a child to write to a worker who is transferred within or leaves the agency, the idea is gaining acceptance. There is less fear that a previous worker will interfere with treatment. Perhaps this is related to social work becoming more mature as a profession, as well as to a better understanding of the dynamics of relationship and treatment in placement. Social workers are having increased experience in interdisciplinary work such as seeing a child in casework interviews while he is also seen in group or conjoint interviewing. Also, there is study of what responsibility should be delegated to the semiprofessional child care workers who play so important a part in a placed child's life. Some adoption agencies now counsel adoptive parents to allow the child to visit or to be visited by his former foster parents; and some residential treatment centers encourage the child to keep in contact with foster parents.[14]

Some workers keep in contact with former clients by seeing them in private practice, or by being available when the child calls, etc. This may be a general policy in some agencies, or more probably, a policy with some workers in some agencies. At any rate, there is not enough planned procedure and guidance to caseworkers and other child care staff leaving an agency as to how they should end a primary relationship with a child, but keep a supportive connection as long as the child needs it.

Procedures to Avoid Traumatic Effects

Attention must be turned to ways of cushioning the impact on the child of a change of worker. To quote Flesch: "It is a professional duty to inquire into the reasons for frequent changes of jobs among social workers and to attempt to improve their situation. Certainly more adequate recognition both through salary and in status would reduce the necessity of caseworkers' having to achieve professional satisfaction in other ways." [15]

Social workers have made progress in salaries and in status recently, but not enough. The administrations of agencies must do more to educate boards and communities about the importance of good personnel practices that will keep staff turnover at a minimum.

Agencies that have several types of facilities under their jurisdiction might avoid changing the worker when a child is transferred from one setting to another. For example, when a child living at home and attending the guidance clinic is transferred to a foster home, the trauma of separation from his own family is bad enough without the trauma of loss of worker as well. Many children regress seriously because they cannot cope with simultaneous, multiple losses. Some would regress less if at least their worker remained constant. Having a worker based in one facility continue to work with a child transferred to another might involve additional expense for travel and in time required for coordination and supervision, but continuation with the same worker might cut down the length of treatment, and thereby reduce cost.

In a situation such as transfer of a child from a foster home to a residential treatment center or vice versa, arrangements might be made for a child to keep his caseworker until he has taken roots in his new surroundings, if it is not possible to make a continuing assignment. Some workers may find traveling to a different setting to see the child a nuisance, but professional workers have a responsibility to examine their investment in therapeutic relationships. "If we grant that we as individuals have created a unique personal situation with a client, then we as individuals have a unique personal responsibility to that client, at least until the change to the next worker is successfully completed." [16]

When a child is transferred from one agency to another, it is the responsibility of both agencies to facilitate the change for the child and to see that the important relationship with his caseworker is not traumatically terminated. Whatever procedures are followed must relate to the specific situation. Care must be taken, of course, to avoid overidentification of the worker with the child, and to help the child relate as rapidly as possible to the new setting and new worker; not to the exclusion of the previous experience, but rather helping the child incorporate its meaning, and move on to a new relationship.

Another way of avoiding a change of worker when either the child or the worker leaves, is to continue treatment in private practice. If a child goes home, it is likely that his family will pay the practitioner directly. If a child is in placement, the agency may pay the fee.[17]

The use of student caseworkers should probably be avoided for children who are likely to be particularly vulnerable to separation experiences. There are advantages, however, that student workers can bring to work with a child. Students are likely to have more time for intensive work, and are constantly under skilled supervision. When a case is assigned to a student, clients and coworkers such as foster mothers should be told that the worker is a student, and will be with the agency a limited time.[18] Reassignment should be planned to allow the student to remain in the picture until the client has made the transition to the new worker. Supervisors are responsible for seeing that a student helps his client to relate to the other people in the agency, and to the agency as such so that there is some continuity of relationships for the client when the student leaves. Clients of students should also know that a student's supervisor knows about them and is available in the absence of the student.

Conclusion

Care for children must be built on sound mental health principles. Cutting ties between worker and child when the worker leaves an agency, or when the child is transferred to a different setting within the same agency, might seem an administrative expedient, but could be detrimental and expensive.

The goal of social work is service to the client. Social workers must be wary that the child does not become a pawn in the game of change. Change of workers out of workers' needs or agencies' needs is a problem "bound up with every question of professional ethics." [19]

The human element is an essential part of the professional relationship. Effective service to child clients depends upon full and wise use of the casework relationship. As Anna Freud has pointed out: "Apparently spontaneous attachments of the children really arise in answer to a feeling in the adult person of which the adult was not aware in the beginning, or the reasons for which only became apparent after some recording." [20] Such emotional stirrings on the part of the adult, when recognized and held under control . . . are of inestimable value." [21]

Social work invests greatly in teaching and in helping caseworkers develop skill in use of the casework relationship. It is time the field examined the losses it incurs through traumatic interruption of this relationship, and developed procedures to ensure that change and separation are growth-producing and not a cause of regression.

Notes and References

1. Sidney Z. Moss and Miriam S. Moss, "When a Caseworker Leaves an Agency: The Impact on Worker and Client," Social Casework, XLVII, No. 7 (1967), 433-437.
2. Regina Flesch, Treatment Considerations in Reassignment of Clients (New York: Family Service Association of America, 1947); Eleanor Pavenstedt and Irene Andessen, "The Uncompromising Demand of a Three-Year-Old for a Real Mother," in The Psychoanalytic Study of the Child, I (London: Hogarth Press, 1945); Helen D. Wallach, "Terminating Treatment as a Loss," in The Psychoanalytic Study of the Child, XVI (New York: International Universities Press, 1961), pp. 538-548.
3. Flesch, op. cit., p. 80.
4. Children of diplomats who are exposed to frequent changes of places of living, neighborhood, schools, etc., often grow up without personal ties.
5. Margaret S. Mahler, "Thoughts About Development and Individuation," in The Psychoanalytic Study of the Child, XVIII (New York: International Universities Press, 1963), pp. 307-324.
6. Selma Fraiberg, "Futher Considerations of the Role of Transference in Latency," in The Psychoanalytic Study of the Child, XXI (New York: International Universities Press, 1966), pp. 213-236.
7. Esther Appelberg, "The Cottage Meeting as a Therapeutic Tool," in Henry W. Maier, ed., Group Work as Part of Residential Treatment (New York: National Association of Social Workers, 1965), pp. 150-151; Morris

Fritz Mayer, 'The Parental Figures in Residential Treatment," Social Service Review, XXXIV, No. 3 (1960), 273-285.

8. Flesch, op. cit., p. 27.

9. Sidney Z. Moss and Miriam S. Moss, op. cit., p. 435.

10. Esther Appelberg, "Verbal Accessibility of Adolescents: A Comparison of Adolescents Living in a Treatment Institution and Adolescents Living in the Community with Their Parents," unpublished doctoral dissertation, Western Reserve University, School of Applied Social Services, Cleveland, 1961. For a shorter version, see Appelberg, "Verbal Accessibility of Adolescents," Child Welfare, XLIII, No. 2 (1964)," 86-90. This conclusion supports findings of earlier works. See Norman A. Polansky and Erwin S. Weiss, "Determinants of Accessibility to Treatment in a Children's Institution," Journal of Jewish Communal Service, XXXVI, No. 2 (1959), 130-137; Norman A. Polansky, Erwin S. Weiss, and Arthur Blum, "Children's Verbal Accessibility as a Function of Content and Personality," American Journal of Orthopsychiatry, XXXI, No. 1 (1961), 153-169; and Arthur Blum and Norman A. Polansky, "Effect on Staff Role of Children's Verbal Accessibility," Social Work, VI, No. 1 (1961), 29-37.

11. Sidney Z. Moss and Miriam S. Moss, op. cit., 433.

12. Appelberg, op. cit., 17.

13. Flesch reports the same experiences, op. cit., p. 42.

14. Placement agencies have changed their rules on parents' visits and have become more flexible because of their understanding of what separation and placement mean to the child.

15. Flesch, op. cit., p. 80.

16. Ibid., p. 80.

17. This proposal fits into the model proposed by Irving Piliavin in "Restructuring the Provision of Social Services," Social Work, XIII, No. 1 (1968), 34.

18. Whether the client should be told that the worker is a student comes up for discussion in every casework course. In many years of teaching, I have found that the majority of students prefer to present themselves as students.

19. Flesch, op. cit.

20. Pavenstedt and Andessen, op.cit.

21. Ibid., 231.

The Significance of Personal Guardianship for Children in Casework

Almost 18 years ago Irving Weissman, discussing the legal guardianship of children, said:

> The responsibility to provide legal guardianship falls to the state under the doctrine of *parens patriae* which, in our American conception, means a state guardianship of children which becomes activated as soon as parents cease fulfilling their obligations toward the child according to the standards of child welfare set by the community. Implicit in this conception of public responsibility for children is the idea that the child is not a chattel to be bought or sold in the black market nor a plaything to be lightly picked up and discarded. He is a human being to be treated with dignity and respect. His removal or permanent transfer from the security of his own family is regarded as a public concern properly subject to public scrutiny and sanction. When need for such a change arises, the state is activated to the role of fiduciary who does not want to possess the child but rather wants to safeguard his status and security by bringing the child into the protection and care of another family setting as soon as possible. But, as the Children's Bureau study points out, the state largely defaults on this obligation to children by failing to

From: *Source Book of Teaching Materials on the Welfare of Children* (New York: Council on Social Work Education, 1969), pp. 60-65. Reprinted with permission.

prohibit the casual passing on of children. In some states, parents are allowed to give up their children in voluntary arrangements. Many states encourage a practice amounting to "finders are keepers" with regard to children by statutes which embody the doctrine of *in loco parentis* in one form or another. This doctrine is widely interpreted to grant guardianship in fact to persons who voluntarily take a child into their own home and thereby stand in the place of parents to the child. The Children's Bureau favors a correlation of laws to eliminate such conflicts and to declare positively and clearly the state's responsibility to protect children who lose their parents. The bureau would place a duty of obtaining legal authorization upon people and agencies who take children into longtime care. It believes that the legal status of a child in relation to the person or agency caring for him should always be made clear but it does not believe that a requirement of a legal guardian for every child would be practicable at this time. It believes, as the study findings show, that in their present stage of development court and social agency resources would be disastrously overtaxed by the vast extension of work that would follow such a requirement.[1]

This last statement is challenged by Alex Elson, a lawyer who discusses Weissman's paper. Elson states:

This is one conclusion with which I cannot agree. It is true that there are considerations of expediency which will impede or perhaps make impossible the realization of the desired goal. But faced with what is beginning to approach a collapse of existing machinery under ever-increasing burdens, I am strongly of the opinion that considerations of expediency should not be permitted to stand in the way of vigorous efforts to bring about reform without further delay. Since there is no disagreement as to the objective to be sought, the effectiveness of a program designed to achieve this objective should not be watered away by an advance conclusion that its accomplishment is impracticable at this time.[2]

In discussing the issue, Weissman further states:

Several problems are presented by agency acceptance of legal guardianship. The relation of guardian and ward is intended to be a personal relationship, and it is questionable whether an agency can stand in the place of parents in the literal sense of the law. The concept that the guardian completes the legal wholeness of the child raises questions as to whether the agency can operate in the role of child representative and professional agency at one and the same time. The contradiction this situation points up is that the agency becomes its own client in that as guardian of the child, it carries the authority to accept, reject, and evaluate its own activities.[3]

Professional Responsibility

Despite Weissman's provocative questions and proposals as to the social work profession's responsibility in legal guardianship for children, his hope that "the questions which I have raised will be carried into agency staff meetings . . ." has not, to my knowledge, materialized.[4, 5, 6, 7] Yet, since I am in agreement with Weissman that the relation of guardian and ward is intended to be personal, I wish to discuss this point and to show its significance for casework. I believe we should discuss with parents the importance of drawing up a will that names a guardian. This follows the tradition of "institutional conception" of social welfare, which suggests that social service provisions are organized and offered even when other institutional arrangements of society are operating well. The concept of guardianship should be introduced to the parents while the family is still functioning well and able to take care of the child.

My primary concern is the protection of the person, not property. Therefore, I address myself to the caseworker in family agencies, child guidance clinics, child welfare agencies, and hospitals.[8]

In major books on child welfare,[9, 10, 11, 12] the issue of guardianship is hardly mentioned. Discussion with practitioners indicates that if a guardian is appointed, it is a guardian for the property and not for the person. In some instances, one guardian may be appointed for the property, and another for the person. The legal actuality differentiates between protection of the person and protection of the property. Such a differentiation is often made by fathers in their wills. The protection of the child is left to the mother; protection of the property is shared with or left entirely to a guardian or trustee.

Why the Concept of Guardianship Is Ignored

The number of children who need guardians is great, and we might have a feeling of defeat before we even start [13] if we were to set as our goal appointment of a guardian for every child for whom agencies have acted *in loco parentis.* Perhaps because we see an agency as assuming the role of guardian, we have felt no need for appointment of a guardian. Despite espousal of the concept that parents retain responsibility and the agency shares in the responsibility for the child's care, we still fall short of acting according to reason and professional conviction. All too often we view parents as disturbing factors in our work, expressed in additional demands on our time and criticisms as to how we deal with their children. This feeling is often shared by all the child care agents: the caseworker, cottage counselor, and foster parent. The feeling is increased when parents work against us, disrupt placement, sabotage our efforts, and negate whatever gains we might have made with the child. It is not surprising that although we put up with the parents out of conviction or necessity, we do not venture to look for new trouble. In other words, why should we appoint a guardian, who might interfere just as much as a parent?

Perhaps even more decisive is the feeling that guardianship is associated, consciously or subconsciously, with death. One names a guardian in anticipation of one's own death. Most people prefer not to think about death, and social workers do not differ in this respect from other humans. Social work literature deals minimally with the issue of death. Although psychoanalytic literature has not done much better, it has devoted more space to this subject in recent years. Yet not many of the theoretical implications of death and mourning, especially in regard to children, seem to have entered our practice.

I have come across few cases where the caseworker has used the concept of guardianship in dealing with his clients. Nor do I know of more than one or two cases where the worker raised this question with the client, even when the situation indicated it was necessary. In cases where parents brought up the question of what would happen to their children after they died, caseworkers have failed to explore this possibility.

One might speculate whether the concept of guardianship is not also a matter influenced by social class. Most social workers come from the lower and middle classes, where designation of guardianship may not have been a tradition. In upper-class families, where property is important, a family that does not designate a guardian is the exception.

Among my own friends, even the professionals, most have done nothing about guardianship. Their reaction has been similar to that of my casework class where, out of 10 students who are parents, only two have made provision for a guardian in their wills. Of the two, one was motivated to this action only after he and his wife were almost killed in an accident. Another student said she had thought about designating a guardian, but did not know how to proceed; after all, how could she explain the designation of a guardian to her children?

Thinking about the possibility of one's death need not be morbid or damaging to one's children, since death is part of life and making provision for such an eventuality is a duty one owes to the living. Furthermore, preparation for this eventuality can be used constructively and be made part of good casework.

The Parents

Many clients come to us because of their children, whether they admit their helplessness openly, or whether they use the child to ask for help for themselves. In some situations, especially when one parent has died or become seriously ill, or when the child is retarded or mentally ill, the question of the parent's death looms large. At times this worry is expressed openly; at other times the idea is so threatening that the client cannot admit it or express it to the worker. With some clients there is perhaps also a superstitious belief that talking about death might make it happen. With some clients, if they start talking about their worry, they may no longer be able to repress it. Despite our own feeling of discomfort and need to deny death, we are often not attuned to the client's fears of death. If we respond, we are likely to do so in terms of what we think are their unconscious feelings toward their spouse or children, e.g., ambivalence or anger, especially if we deal with persons who seem to be in reasonable health. The client, like all of us, has real reasons to think about his death, and he should be encouraged to make provision for the living, who are his responsibility. The client can be worked with on both levels: (1) to explore his feelings; (2) to make reasonable provision in the form of a will. Once steps toward a will and appointment of a guardian have taken place, the client's energy will be freed so that his family relationships can be explored in greater depth. There are, of course, clients and situations where exploration of the feelings have to take place before clients can take steps to draw up a will.

There are parents who feel ambivalent and predominantly hostile toward their children and who fear their children's ambivalence and hostility toward them. The parents might be threatened by appointing a rival, so to speak, for the affection of their children. In such cases there might be an almost primitive feeling of magic; by drawing up a will, they bring about what their children wish upon them. In these cases we have to help the client work through his feelings; the drawing up of a will is evidence of integration of his insight.

In cases where one parent has died, or where one is sick, or where the child is retarded or mentally ill, a parent may experience a sense of relief through making provision for guardianship.

The agency should always point out that it would step in and take care of the child, should something happen to the parent. In one case a mother, recently widowed, expressed to her worker in the guidance clinic her fear as to what would happen to her 10-year-old son should she die. The mother had asked for help shortly after the death of her husband. She was greatly relieved when the worker pointed out to her that should she die, the worker, with the help of the agency, would make all necessary provisions for her son. Once reassured, this mother was freed to enter into treatment, deal with her grief, and look into her attitudes and feelings toward her son.

Relative or Friend as Guardian

Work with this mother could have been carried further by getting her to explore who were the relatives close to or interested in the child who might be willing to take him into their home. This would have enabled the mother to share her fears with her family. This could have led to one of them expressing willingness to take the child and look after him. In many instances a relative or friend is willing to take over some of the functions of a parent. He might be the one who would apply on behalf of the child to the agency, in event of the parent's illness or death. He might be the one who would take the child into his home temporarily, until a permanent placement is worked out. Thus an additional trauma of temporary placement in a strange home might be avoided. He might also be the one who would feel morally obligated to maintain regular contact with the child once he is placed, thus assuring the presence of some familiar, significant person. Thus placement would not mean, as too frequently it does, total separation from all that is familiar. It might also mean that the child would have a place to go for vacation and that he would be visited by his guardian and not feel the terrible loneliness of many children whose parents have died or who have been hospitalized for years. Implicit in this concept of guardianship is the idea that the guardian should be somebody familiar and close with whom the child has developed some feeling of trust and with whom he feels comfortable. We shall come back to this point and how this can be explained to the child.

How this idea helped another client is illustrated in this example:

Mrs. S. is the adoptive mother of a 14-year-old, mildly retarded girl who is in a class for children of retarded mental development. The father died a year before the mother came to the agency. She showed that she had not been able to accept the retardation of her adopted daughter and was seeking to place the blame. Had she been cheated by the agency, or had she done the damage? Yet she also asked for help in controlling herself in her hostile behavior to her daughter. She was unable to set limits for her daughter, who lately had started to ignore her, to spite and fight her. In an interview with the caseworker, Mrs. S. told how her daughter had become upset when she, the mother, became sick. "What will happen to me if you should die, too?" The mother had given the usual reassurance—that she just had a cold and that she would not die, since people don't die from colds. That this had not reassured the girl became quickly evident as further exploration showed that her daughter's behavior became worse. Toward the end of the interview, the mother was able to say that she, too, was worried about what would happen to her daughter should she die. This worry had started after the death of her husband and had increased since her recent illness.

There were many ways in which the worker could have responded. The mother's feelings of ambivalence toward her adopted daughter, her anger toward her husband who died, could have been examined. The worker chose to point up that the worry of the daughter and herself were real, even though the mother was in good health. When further discussion showed that the mother had no close relatives, she was encouraged to think about close friends, and their willingness to be guardian. The worker pointed out that the agency would assume the responsibility and place the child if a close friend would not take her. On the other hand, it would be helpful to the child if the friend would work together with the agency, be informed about the child's progress, and keep in contact with the girl. The mother explored the idea with two close friends. One agreed to be the guardian. Although she would not take the child, she said she would keep in contact with the agency, visit the child in placement, and invite her to her house for the holidays. The mother was also helped to discuss the matter with the child, after the worker had paved the way with the child directly. The mother informed the girl about the steps she had taken with the agency and her friend, and encouraged the girl to discuss her worry with the agency, and to get better acquainted with her mother's friend. In casework, the mother was able to relinquish her unreal idealization of her husband, to express her anger that he had left her alone to cope with their daughter. She was also able to express her disappointment and anger that he had not made a will and that it had taken a lot of time, trouble, and effort to straighten out financial affairs. The support the mother was given to make concrete provisions for her daughter—things her husband had not done for her and the child—increased her self-esteem as a woman and mother. Her facing of reality by words and action strengthened her, and enabled her eventually to work through her feelings about herself and her daughter. This led to improvement in their relationship.

In another case, Mr. and Mrs. B. had been coming for almost 2 years to an agency where their 13-year-old daughter, afflicted with mongolism, was receiving special education. They often worried about what would happen to the daughter were they to die. At times they said that their son (21 years old) would take care of her. Perhaps the B.s not only were concerned as to what would happen to their daughter should they die, but may have had the wish that their daughter would die, a wish they could not express even to themselves. Yet their concern was real, and was accessible to treatment. The parents were informed about state institutions, and also were helped to discuss the matter directly with their son. The son did not agree to have his sister live with him, but he agreed to be the guardian, arrange for institutionalization and keep close contact with her, should the parents no longer be able to take care of her. Thus they were able to take some comfort in that they had faced the question openly with their son and had taken all possible steps to insure the future of their daughter.

The Child

At times it is not enough to work only with the parents. Often even if they are willing, they are unable to face the question with their child and to discuss the possibility of their death. Yet they may have made provisions so that the child would not be left alone. In such a situation, if the parents permit, we should work directly with the child.

Children are much more worried about death than adults usually are ready to admit. Anna Freud pointed out that all children over 2 years old, during the London blitz, knew that people were being killed or getting hurt by bombs and falling houses.[14] In her opinion even such young children have a concept of death. Yet since the child's grief is short-lived, "observers seldom appreciate the depth and seriousness of this grief of a small child." "Mourning of equal intensity in an adult person would have to run its course throughout a year; the same process in the child between 1 and 2 years will normally be over in 36 to 48 hours." [15] Anna Freud explains that the difference in the duration is due to psychological differences between the child and the adult. The child's life is governed by the pleasure principle: "Its memories of the past are spoilt by the disappointment which it feels at the present moment. It has no outlook into the future. . . ." [16] That some children do not seem to have a concept of death and do not seem to mourn is explained by Robert Furman as these particular children's incapacity for mourning. "When Lindemann's (1944) observation revealed the total inability of some adults to grieve . . . there was no suggestion the adults were incapable of grief." [17]

The children's concept of death and ability to mourn are related to age, developmental level, and individual dynamics, as are their fears of death; e.g., during the oedipal and adolescent periods, fear of desertion and death is heightened. Yet apart from the child's inner reality is an outer reality of which children are much aware. Children know that pets and animals die; they know that people die. They have seen dying soldiers on television, they hear about plane accidents, they read about death in books, and often they are exposed to the death of a relative, a friend of the family, or they know about a death in the family of a schoolmate. If they are allowed to, it is only expected that they will ask, "Should mommy and daddy also die, what would happen to me?"

Death of a national hero, who also represents a father image, influences the child's inner dynamics to a degree depending on the child's sense of security and his stage of personality development.[18] We all became aware of this when President Kennedy was assassinated. Alpert, in discussing children's reactions to the assassination, found that a "marked shift in defenses seen in the therapeutic sessions leaves no doubt as to the anxiety-arousing effect of the events." [19] Reaction of my friends' children to the assassination of Dr. Martin Luther King, Jr., demonstrated this point again.

Since death is always a reality in children's lives, the concept of death should be discussed with them in words they can understand even before they come into close contact with the death of a particularly significant person.[20] The will and the provisions that have been made for them could be part of this process if they ask what would happen in the event of the parents' death. We know of several cases where parents, young and healthy, have discussed this with their children, without observable ill effects. On the contrary, we believe that the children have been strengthened in their ability to cope with reality, to discuss painful feelings openly, and to live with less fear. We think that these children have gained some inner security.

Not all children will respond positively. Initially some may react with heightened anxiety. The degree of anxiety will depend on the parent-child relation, the child's sense of trust, the developmental level, and the adjustment of the child. Implied is that whenever the caseworker is called in, he should know these dynamics thoroughly.

Marjorie McDonald,[21] discussing the effect on nursery school children of the death of the mother of one of them, reports that those children who mastered the trauma most successfully wondered what would happen to the child who experienced the loss. They also asked whether "their mothers or they themselves might die."

How the social worker can help the child cope with fear of death and to understand the concept of guardianship is shown in the following illustration, a continuation of the case of the adoptive mother of the retarded child, discussed earlier.

The worker told the child that she had heard from the mother how concerned she was that the mother, like the father, would die. The worker pointed out that although the mother was in good health, nobody was immune from death. Yet to meet this remote possibility, the mother had made provisions that the child would not be left alone —the mother's friend and the agency would take care of her. Thus, in simple words during a few interviews, the worker spelled out provisions made for care of the girl. This enabled the child to free herself to a great degree of worry about a lonely future. Since the worker was aware and acceptant of the girl's grief, this enabled the child to express for the first time her sorrow over her father and her feelings of desertion. Then the worker was able to discuss with the child her feelings about being adopted, and leave the child with some positive feeling about her biological mother. She pointed out that her biological mother, who could not take care of her, had made provisions for her by bringing her to an adoption agency. The agency had placed her with adoptive parents so she could have the home her biological mother could not give her. Now her adoptive mother had made provision for the future. The agency had promised to help her should anything happen to her mother. Concretizing and understanding the concept of guardianship, knowing that if something should happen to the mother, she would not be left to fend for herself, reassured the girl about present and future, and reduced anxiety and fear. The difficulties mother and daughter experienced in their relationship were greatly alleviated, and both were able to live with greater trust in each other.

Conclusion

The concept of guardianship for children is important. In casework we have not used it or explored its possibilities sufficiently. Whether and when the personal guardian should also be the guardian of property is also an important question. The client's or agency's lawyer should be consulted if necessary, so that the child will have all possible protection. The Legal Aid Society could be a resource here. The Bar Association could be asked to cooperate. There may be ways to introduce the human implications into the curriculums of law schools. Social workers could alert lawyers to the emotional implications of the guardianship issue for parent and child. Thus lawyers could refer clients to a family agency or child guidance clinic, which would help parents to discuss guardianship with children. Many children come from such disrupted families that it would not be possible to find a guardian. But perhaps here we react sometimes out of our own prejudices. Working with disrupted and poverty-stricken families, we do not think that there might be a member who is interested or whose concern might be aroused. Thus agencies, perhaps out of pressure, despair, or lack of conviction, have not done enough to introduce this concept to their clients. Yet "today in the United States, the means are available to permit the welfare of the child, not his estate, to determine the social and legal provisions made for him." [22] The children of the poor have a right to know that they will be taken care of should disaster befall their parents. Taylor's [23] proposal for subsidized guardianship merits serious thought. To all parents who come for help with their child, the concept of guardianship should be introduced—many will be open to such a proposal. Through this proposal the worker demonstrates his view of the parent as the primary source of continuing responsibility for the child. The parent, by such a step, gains strength and affirmation in his parenting. In all cases where parents have to place children, or where there is illness in the family, the possibility of guardianship should be explored, to help the client obtain a guardian. Social workers in hospitals should especially be attuned to the patient's need in this respect. Although fear may be evoked initially, many parents ultimately experience relief if the question of will and guardianship for their children is discussed with them.

Although today we have fewer orphans than in the 19th Century, we have many more single parents, and a new generation of half-orphans, the children of soldiers killed in Vietnam and other places. Every one-parent family should be helped to obtain a guardian.[24]

The agency, acting *in loco parentis*, is not always enough; some hospitals will not hospitalize a child unless a personal guardian signs the child in. They will not accept the agency as custodian, but insist that the agency go to court and a personal guardian be appointed. If property is involved, a guardian must always be appointed.[25] Appointment of a guardian when the agency has placed a child whose parents are dead may help to develop or strengthen kinship ties and meaningful friendships. It may also be helpful to children whose parents have disappeared, or children who have been hospitalized for years. It will help the child keep normal contacts with the community at large, and lessen the impact of institutionalization.

The concrete steps of making these provisions will relieve some parents from real worries and ease some children's fears. Parents should be helped to inform their children about such plans, and to see to it that the children and their guardians become well acquainted. An older child should be asked his preference as to a guardian. If necessary the worker, with permission of the parents, should discuss plans directly with the child.

The agency should view the guardian as a helping person who now, too, is *in loco parentis*, and should keep contact with him. Where the family cannot find a relative or friend willing to be the guardian, the agency should seek a suitable person in the community willing to serve in this role. It might not be possible to find guardians for all children, but all possibilities should be explored. The community has to be tapped for resources.

Notes and References

1. Irving Weissman, "Legal Guardianship of Children?" in The Social Welfare Forum, 1950, official proceedings, 77th Annual National Conference of Social Work (New York: Columbia University Press, 1950), pp. 85 ff.
2. Ibid., p. 94.
3. Ibid., p. 89.
4. How to Provide for Their Future, pamphlet published by the National Association for Retarded Children.

5. See Alan Keith-Lucas' discussion of Weissman's paper in The Social Welfare Forum, 1950, ibid., pp. 95-100.
6. Legislative Guides for the Termination of Parental Rights and Responsibilities and the Adoption of Children (Washington, D.C.: U.S. Department of Health, Education, and Welfare, Children's Bureau Publication No. 394, 1961).
7. Standards for Services of Child Welfare Institutions. (New York: Child Welfare League of America, 1964), p. 100.
8. A thought-provoking proposal is that of Hasseltine B. Taylor: "Guardianship or Permanent Placement of Children," California Law Review, LIV, No. 2 (1966), 741-747. She suggests financially subsidized guardianship for children not free for adoption but in need of long-term foster care. These guardians would no longer be accountable to the Department of Welfare. Since guardianship, instead of permanent placement or permanent foster homes, takes the agency out of the picture, it would mean that agencies could devote their services more efficiently to those children and their families who really cannot do without them.
9. Henrietta Gordon. Casework Services for Children: Principles and Practices (Boston: Houghton Mifflin, 1956).
10. Alfred J. Kahn. Planning Community Services for Children in Trouble (New York: Columbia University Press, 1963).
11. Alfred Kadushin, Child Welfare Services (New York: Macmillan Co., 1967), p. 52.
12. Harold E. Simmons. Protective Services for Children: A Public Social Welfare Responsibility (General Welfare Publications, Sacramento, Calif., 1968).
13. In 1960 about 3 percent of the nation's children were living with neither parent, but with relatives, in institutions, or in foster homes. Kadushin, ibid., p. 52.
14. Anna Freud and Dorothy Burlingham, War and Children (New York: International Universities Press, 1945), pp. 15-16.
15. Ibid., p. 51.
16. Ibid., pp. 51-52.
17. Robert A. Furman, "Death and the Young Child: Some Preliminary Considerations," in The Psychoanalytic Study of the Child, Vol. XIX (New York International Universities Press, 1964), 321 ff.
18. For a discussion on similarities and differences in children's and adolescents' reaction to loss of a parent and loss of a hero see Martha Wolfenstein, "Death of a President: Children's Reaction to Two Kinds of Loss," in Children and the Death of a President. (New York: Anchor Books).
19. August Alpert, "A Brief Communication on Children's Reaction to the Assassination of the President," The Psychoanalytic Study of the Child, Vol. XIX, ibid., pp. 313 ff.
20. In her conclusion about the multi-disciplinary studies about children and the death of a president, Wolfenstein states: ". . . it was for them (for

young adolescents) an initiation into the experience of painful loss which none escapes in life. Perhaps this expression of grief . . . will have prepared them to some extent to tolerate later losses." Children and the Death of a President, ibid., p. 207.

21. Marjorie McDonald, "A Study of the Reaction of Nursery School Children to the Death of a Child's Mother," The Psychoanalytic Study of the Child, Vol. XIX, ibid., pp. 358.

22. Taylor, California Law Review, ibid., p. 5.

23. Taylor, ibid.

24. There are also the questions of war pensions and other benefits that may be of great importance, especially for these children.

25. We are more concerned about property than about life; society had laws about the protection of property long before there were laws for protection of the child, whether these were child labor laws, or laws relating to child abuse. We still struggle with the concept that the child is the property of its parents.

Physical Illness in the Residential Treatment Center

Residential treatment centers for children may vary in their theoretical frameworks of reference and in their practices. Some emphasize the therapeutic hour; others emphasize the therapeutic milieu. They all agree, however, that the use of the structured environment is basic to the residential treatment of children. Such agreement is the obvious justification for separating the child from his home and placing him in the residential setting.

Lack of Available Information

In surveying the literature on the subject of residential treatment, however, one is struck with the absence of references to physical illness, its possible meaning, and its treatment in the therapeutic milieu. The nurse is hardly mentioned at all. Even more puzzling is the omission of any reference to physical health or illness or to the nurse in the literature directed toward the education of the child care worker. The exceptions to this advocate that the child care staff should have training that will help them to understand health problems and that "children who are ill should be cared for in surroundings that are

---

Published originally in CHILD WELFARE, XLV, 8, October 1966.

familiar to them, so long as this is medically and socially desirable." [1]
Although one can find discussions about everyday life, one will seek
in vain for consideration of the meaning of a child's physical complaints and illness or the role of the child care worker in handling
these important everyday problems.

Many of us who are concerned with child welfare have become so
preoccupied with the emotional problems of the child that we have
forgotten or overlooked the importance of the physical body in the
lives of our children.[2] We have overlooked physical health or illness
as a part of normal development or as the continuation of previous
attempts to cope with stress. We have failed to perceive illness as
possibly reflecting new symptoms that enable children in treatment to
cope with or defend against new stress. Thus, in residential treatment,
instead of unifying the psyche and the soma and treating the child
as a whole, as one person, we have continually kept these two apart
as if the twain never shall meet.

One exception occurs in the writings of Bettelheim. He discusses
how the appearance and disappearance of physical symptoms in
emotionally disturbed children represent stages in the integrative
process of the readjustment of severely disturbed children in the
Sonia Shankman Orthogenic School. Some children are able to give
up these symptoms; others acquire physical symptoms as a new and
more integrated way of dealing with old and new stress.[3] In the story
of "Harry, a Delinquent Boy," Bettelheim presents the case of one boy
in the Orthogenic School and the role that somatic symptoms play in
his illness and in his recovery.[4] Although he gives some attention to
the role of the nurse, one wishes that he had discussed her role more
fully. Equally neglected is the place of the "sickroom" in this therapeutic milieu.

In 1949, Anna Freud pointed out that if a child is removed from his
home and placed in an environment where the adults are not involved
in the neurotic struggle, the child's symptoms would disappear for
some time until newer, meaningful adults were involved by the child
in the neurosis.[5] Bettelheim, too, points out how a majority of the children lost most of their physical symptoms after being in his school for
a year and how some of these symptoms appeared only in connection
with home visits or visits of these children's parents.[6] He discusses
why these children needed these symptoms and why they were able

to let go of them in the course of treatment, but he does not discuss the symptoms that might result from the new neurotic involvement with caretaking people to which Anna Freud refers. He also fails to examine how helping persons could influence these physical symptoms and their underlying causes through more conscious use of the whole treatment staff within the therapeutic milieu.

Writers who discuss the concept of transference to parental figures in residential treatment offer illustrations that deal with behavior problems only and neglect the soma. For example, in an excellent discussion of psychotherapy in residential treatment, Krug discusses the function of the child care worker who carries out many of the usual parental functions and says that "because of the intimate living experience having to do with eating, toileting, sleeping, playing and learning, children will look upon these [child care] workers as parent figures." [7] And in her third principle of psychotherapy, Krug states:

> ". . . within the security of the therapeutic relationship, the child's emotional development is recapitulated in a new, corrective manner for meeting his needs for both dependency and growth . . . but children with greater disturbances in ego function and with marked pregenital fixations require repetitive demonstrations of their acceptance through important daily experiences, especially those having to do with bodily functions. . . . Through the daily experiences residential workers have many opportunities to demonstrate to the child these concrete evidences of acceptance. As a result these children sometimes develop their first meaningful relationships in residence rather than in individual therapy." [8]

Yet, no mention is made of the parental functions of the child care worker when physical sickness affects the children, nor is any attention given to the integration of this concern in the design of the therapeutic milieu.

Although some residential treatment centers are making every effort to keep the mildly sick or injured child in the cottage, others send the child—even with a minor illness—to the infirmary or sickroom.[9] If we really believe this principle of psychotherapy, how can we justify removing the physically ill child from the cottage and relieving —or depriving—the child care worker of any responsibility? Do we not undermine our efforts to give the child the much needed acceptance, warmth, and familiarity in the stress and tension of physical illness and, in fact, contradict ourselves by failing to provide concrete evidences of acceptance? Do we not instead *provide* an experience of rejection by not placing responsibility for physical care of the sick child on the cottage staff?

The Child and the Infirmary

The rationale for the cottage system is known. Yet, what happens to the child who complains that he does not feel well? He is usually sent to the infirmary, where his temperature is taken and where he is kept during school, for the day, overnight, or for a few days. Babcock has pointed to the adult patient's fear of abandonment, a fear that the adult is not aware of, since it relates to the fear of abandonment that he experienced in his childhood.[10] For the child in placement—who is experiencing abandonment by his parents who deserted him—abandonment is not an infantile fear, as in the case of the hospitalized adult, but a very real one. By again removing him from the parental figure, i.e., the cottage worker, we repeat his original trauma—this at a time when "he has a great need for reassurance by people who 'belong' to him and also by persons unrelated to him but upon whom he is economically, physically, and emotionally dependent." [11] Thus, at a time when he needs his substitute parent most urgently, he is removed from him and from the cottage life that is supposed to give him some semblance of living in a home and is the basis of the therapeutic design of residential treatment.

This separation from the cottage takes place at a time when the hurt might be part of a normal childhood illness, an attention-getting device, or an avoidance of dealing with the everyday stresses that are part of emotional maturing. Even though we might recognize these underlying dynamics in the child's behavior and might talk about his need to regress, we continue to deal with them from the point of view of administrative expediency. Somehow if the body is involved, the child no longer belongs in the cottage, but in the infirmary. We do not ask ourselves how removal from the cottage influences the child's psyche at a time when he needs more intensive bodily care, or how his physical illness affects his "psychology" and self-image.

Nurse-Child Relationship

In the infirmary, the child might then look at the nurse who devotes herself to him as a positive parental figure, whereas the cottage counselor who deserted and rejected him becomes even more invested with negative feelings.[12] Having found the good parent in the nurse, he is now in a conflict situation—unwilling to get better and to leave the infirmary to return to the bad parent in the cottage. He does not want to move out of his regression and leave the security of the bed.

Many nurses are very sensitive to the child's psychological and physical needs, but we know little about what goes on between the nurse and the child, especially in terms of how much understanding and consideration she gives to the child's psychological needs while dealing with his physical needs. All we hear is that children "love" or "hate" to go to the infirmary, but this, of course, tells us nothing.

It is apparent that we know very little about the role of the nurse, how she fits into the treatment center, and how the child perceives her. In two studies, attempts were made to determine whom, among the adults in residential treatment centers, the child considered his confidant.[13] Caseworkers and cottage counselors were named most often, and teachers and administrative staff received some mention, but the nurse was not mentioned once by the children.[14]

Isolation of the Child

We have also failed to take into consideration the way in which the infirmary isolates the child from his peers and how it affects the child. If he is rejected by his peers, a physically ill child may lie in the infirmary for days without being visited by his cottage group. Sometimes the cottage counselor cannot find the time for a visit to the infirmary. Thus, confinement in the infirmary may be perceived by the child as another rejection by his peers and the parent substitute. This may, in turn, increase his negative transference.[15] Physical complaints may be used as part of the struggle with the caretaking adults or with the child's peers. Having been allowed in the infirmary to regress and to revert to behavior inappropriate for his age, he is now unwilling to give up these secondary gains. He becomes involved in a new struggle with his peers and the child care workers who are not willing to tolerate this and want him to give up his now inappropriate behavior and demands. The illness may even be prolonged to continue the struggle.

All these speculations and many others will persist in plaguing us so long as we continue to remove sick children from the cottage, thereby surrendering an opportunity to learn about transference and somatic symptoms in residential treatment.

Why We Are Neglecting the Problem

There are various reasons why we ignore the nurse and fail to give professional consideration to appropriate use of the infirmary. For one thing, there is a lack of understanding that childhood illnesses are part of normal growth and represent something every mother has to cope with in bringing up her children. Furthermore, there is fear that the child care worker might not know how to handle physical illness and that other children might be contaminated. And there are questions of administrative expediency as well as questions of cost.

Consideration should be given to Hartmann's concept of illness and its relationship to reality adaptation so that we may understand how taking care of these inevitable occurrences in growth belongs to cottage life as part of the child's experience in growing up.[16] Moreover, many child care workers have taken care of the physical illnesses of their own children and have done it well.[17] And in the residential treatment center, some child care workers occasionally relieve the nurse. If they can relieve the nurse in the infirmary and if they can take care of their own children, why can they not care for the sick child in the cottage? With respect to contamination of other children, by the time the disease is diagnosed as contagious, the sick child's peers in the cottage or in the school have usually already been exposed. Foster parents are asked to take care of the foster child who has a cold or the measles, even though there are other children in the home. Why should the same not apply to the child in residence?

The arguments for maintaining present arrangements because of administrative expediency and cost are not supportable, because administrative expediency is no justification for poor practice. A therapeutic milieu must start with an administration built not on expediency, but on sound mental health principles.

The National Center for Health Statistics has not collected financial statistics about medical treatment of children in residential centers nor about children living at home who are treated in outpatient clinics.[18] Therefore, we do not know whether there would necessarily be increased cost in operating a residential center for children if physically ill children were cared for in the cottage. In any case, the American Association for Children's Residential Treatment Centers is endeavoring to change the Hill-Burton Act so that Federal funds will be available for changes such as those advocated here. And the Children's Bureau is working on initiating a study on the housing situation in child care institutions in order to change Section 703 of Public Law 88443 (1964) so that funds may be included for building 24-hour children's institutions.

Such excellent efforts are directed to financing, but the changes indicated here are not only a question of money. Attitudes are also important, and no real changes will occur so long as the prevailing attitude is one that holds that the primary deficiencies of the centers' medical programs are "unsatisfactory infirmary facilities, lack of medical followup, and insufficient medical staff." [19]

Certainly, keeping the sick child in the cottage is a complicated matter. For example, the question of contagion cannot be ignored, and there are times when the child has to be removed for this reason. Some child care workers might experience new stresses with this additional responsibility, or they might experience a countertransference in regard to bodily illness.[20] The problem of work schedules could be affected, since the needs of the physically ill child might not coincide with regular duty hours. Arrangements for overtime pay or substitute coverage might have to be worked out. Although somewhat less desirable, substitute coverage would keep the child in his own bed, in his own cottage, and with his own peers.

Benefits of Care Rendered in the Cottage

Since the cottage is, in effect, the child's home, even the most rejected child will feel less rejected in his own room than if he is transferred to the infirmary. In his room, he continues to see his roommates; he keeps in touch with his cottage peers who come to look for their friends and who sometimes stop to ask him how he is or to talk with him. Staying in the cottage also gives the peer group and the adults in charge of the peer group an opportunity to be of some influence upon the sick child. This opportunity is apparently forgotten in our consideration of the practical function of the therapeutic milieu.[21] But, it should not be underestimated when we talk about the influence of the peer group.

In addition, keeping the child in his cottage prevents a child in placement from developing a distorted picture of how one takes care of a sick member of the family or the group. He will recognize that sickness does not inevitably mean being sent away from home, nor does it necessarily mean that at a time of great need, those closest to him will abandon him to strangers. Furthermore, the "healthy child" in the cottage will not be plagued by fears that he, too, will be abandoned should he come down with a cold. Being free of this fear will be helpful in enabling the child to involve himself in a positive relationship with the caretaking person.

The care the sick child needs and gets in the cottage will satisfy some basic needs common to all human beings, especially a sick child. Our providing this care will yield greater understanding and insight into the dynamics of somatic illness, and it might teach us how to deal with children more helpfully. We might learn how to encourage children to give up physical symptoms more quickly, and we might find new avenues of dealing with the sick child. Lodging responsibility for the sick child in the cottage will also intensify relationships with nurses and pediatricians, thus making them an integral part of the treatment plan.

Concluding Comments

There is no question but that rethinking and restudy might involve new administrative problems and, perhaps, additional expenditures. Today we are building new residential treatment centers and reviewing and rebuilding old ones. Some centers continue in the old, comfortable ways; infirmaries, which are costly buildings, are part and parcel of their new residential plants. It is time to raise the question of whether we want to take a new look and find a better way of dealing with old problems. Infirmaries and other community medical facilities certainly are needed for particular children who require isolation because of suicidal or other destructive tendencies, or for certain illnesses that require highly specialized care. But the majority of somatic complaints and illnesses can be looked after in the cottage. This can be done by having additional coverage, providing special sickrooms in each cottage, and including the nurse and an understanding of her role in the training of the child care worker. Staff development programs should include the discussion of childhood diseases and the administering of first aid. The new arrangement for retaining sick children in the cottage can be facilitated by more systematically including nurses and pediatricians in the theoretical and practical framework of the residential center.[22]

The change we advocate here is a change in arrangements and procedures.[23] In a therapeutic milieu, however, arrangements and procedures have significant dynamic consequences. Surely this change can have profound implications for some troubled children. It should, therefore, be carefully considered.

Notes and References

1. CWLA Standards for Services of Child Welfare Institutions (New York: Child Welfare League of America, 1964), p. 52. See also Morris Fritz Mayer, A Guide for Child-care Workers (New York: Child Welfare League of America, 1958), pp. 85-88.
2. In her presentation to the Citizens' Committee for Children, Anna Freud addressed herself to this preoccupation and elaborated on the reasons for this before an audience of lawyers, educators, and pediatricians. See Anna Freud, Psychoanalytic Knowledge of the Child and Its Application to Children's Services, mimeographed (New York: Citizens' Committee for Children, 1964).
3. Bruno Bettelheim and Emmy Sylvester, "Physical Symptoms in Emotionally Disturbed Children" in Psychoanalytic Study of the Child, III/IV (New York: International Universities Press, 1949), 353-391.

4. Bruno Bettelheim, Truants from Life (New York: The Free Press, 1955),˙pp. 389-471.

5. Anna Freud, Psycho-Analytical Treatment of Children (London: Imago Publishing Co., 1946).

6. Bettelheim, op. cit., p. 378.

7. Othilda Krug, "The Applications of Child Psychotherapy in Residential Treatment," American Journal of Psychiatry, CVIII (1952), 695.

8. Ibid., p. 696.

9. From personal communications and observations, we know that in most residential centers, removal of the child for even minor illness is standard practice; written information on this subject is not clear. In a recent study [Lydia F. Hylton, The Residential Treatment Center: Children, Programs, and Costs (New York: Child Welfare League of America, 1964)], only 1 center out of 21 centers reported that it had a sickroom available in every cottage; another reported that it had such a room in every new cottage. Some centers reported having infirmaries or sickrooms either as separate buildings or as part of one cottage. Other centers did not have such facilities at all. Although this study gives us a picture of the medical staff and the medical facilities on the grounds and those used off grounds, we do not know how these centers treat the child when he falls sick. Is he kept in the cottage, or is he sent to the sickroom, to the infirmary, or to a community facility? At what point does the medical staff play what part in contributing to the treatment of the child?

10. Charlotte G. Babcock, "Inner Stress in Illness and Disability," in Howard J. Parad and Roger R. Miller, eds., Ego-Oriented Casework: Problems and Perspectives (New York: Family Service Association of America, 1963), p. 57.

11. Ibid.

12. Children in placement often received very inadequate care by their parents at times of illness.

13. Arthur Blum and Norman A. Polansky, "Effect of Staff Role on Children's Verbal Accessibility," Social Work, VI (1961), pp. 29-37; and Esther Appelberg, Verbal Accessibility of Adolescents. A Comparison of Adolescents Living in a Treatment Institution and Adolescents Living in the Community with their Parents, unpublished doctoral dissertation (Cleveland, Ohio: School of Applied Social Sciences, Western Reserve University, 1961).

14. One has to recognize that in this kind of popularity polling, the discrepancy is more apparent than real, since the odds of choosing an adult confidant from the cottage staff as against the nurse were higher. But the omission is still worth some thought, because most children had frequent contact with the nurse either as outpatients or as patients while they were hospitalized in the infirmary.

15. For further explanation of the concept of transference toward the personnel in a treatment center, see Esther Appelberg, "The Cottage

Meeting as a Therapeutic Tool," in Henry W. Maier, ed., Group Work as Part of Residential Treatment (New York: National Association of Social Workers, 1965), pp. 142-154.

16. See Heinz Hartmann, Essays on Ego Psychology (New York: International Universities Press, 1964), p. 6.

17. Hylton, op. cit., pp. 72-75. Eleven out of 21 centers did not have nurses on their staff. We might, therefore, rightly assume that sick children are not necessarily cared for by nurses, but by the cottage worker performing nursing tasks in the infirmary or in the sickroom.

18. Personal correspondence to the author from E. E. Bryant, Chief, Institutional Population Survey Branch, Division of Health Records Statistics. In the same letter, Mr. Bryant points out that his office plans to do so.

19. Hylton, op. cit., p. 207.

20. Emma N. Plank and Carla Horwood, "Leg Amputation in a Four-Year-Old: Reactions of the Child, Her Family, and the Staff," in Psychoanalytic Study of the Child, XVI (New York: International Universities Press, 1961), 405-422.

21. The importance of the cottage milieu in residential treatment has been studied by Howard W. Polsky [Cottage Six (New York: Russell Sage Foundation, 1962)].

22. For these and other suggestions, see CWLA Standards for Services of Child Welfare Institutions.

23. Those interested in this problem might care to consult the literature that deals with pediatric hospitalization in psychiatric treatment or the literature about pediatric wards. See, for example, Paul C. Laybourne and Herbert C. Miller, "Pediatric Hospitalization of Psychiatric Patients: Diagnostic and Therapeutic Implications," American Journal of Orthopsychiatry, XXXII (1962), 596-603; and Emma N. Plank, Working with Children in Hospitals (Cleveland, Ohio: The Press of Western Reserve University, 1962).

Verbal Accessibility of Adolescents

The purpose of this exploratory field study—part of a larger research project concerned with the problem of "accessibility to treatment" [1]—was to compare two groups of Jewish boys and girls on five variables. This paper, however, will be restricted to the presentation of some of the major findings concerning the following three variables: [2] (1) verbal accessibility of the person, (2) verbal accessibility of the attitudes, and (3) the differential communication pattern with important people—or "target persons"—in their surroundings.

One group, consisting of 30 boys and 14 girls, was drawn from the adolescent population at Bellefaire Residential Treatment Center; the other, consisting of 31 boys and 21 girls who were living with their parents, was drawn from the membership of the B'nai B'rith Youth Organization. For further analysis, each major group was subdivided according to sex. Although the two groups differed with regard to their need for treatment in a residential treatment center, they were matched according to age, sex, and demographic factors of the parents.

Verbal accessibility has been defined as the ability to discuss important attitudes with others. There is a clear conceptual distinction, though, between verbal accessibility of the person and verbal accessibility of the attitude. The former refers to the individual's particular

Published originally in CHILD WELFARE, XLIII, 2, February 1964.

pattern of communication; the latter, to attitudes the expression of which is the norm for a given group.

Attitudes can be graded on a continuum ranging from determinant to dependent. Determinant attitudes influence the way in which individuals function. They are basic, they are formed early in life, and they are typically unconscious; from these, dependent attitudes are derived. A change in determinant attitudes will bring about a change or modification of the personality.

To obtain data, self-avowed verbal accessibility scales—for example, "To whom would you talk about what you think of your mother as a housekeeper?"—were used with all of the adolescents in the study. In addition, the ratings of caseworkers and the rankings of cottage staff were used for the Bellefaire adolescents as independent measures of verbal accessibility. When the results of the self-avowed verbal accessibility scales were correlated with the ratings obtained from the caseworkers and the cottage staff, all three measures showed significant relationships. Not only did they prove the validity of the self-avowed verbal accessibility scales, but they also supported the theory that a person's verbal accessibility is a stable characteristic of the personality that fluctuates only within certain limits. In other words, those children who scored high on the self-avowed verbal accessibility scale were considered to be verbally accessible by the cottage staff and the caseworkers. While this does not mean that they talk equally to every member of the staff, it does mean that in each instance the child maintains a similar position relative to other children.[3] When we compared length of stay in the institution with verbal accessibility, however, no correlation was found.

Comparison of Families

A comparison of the demographic variables measured in this study [4] revealed that the two samples matched each other on parents' country of origin and father's education. They did not, however, match each other in socioeconomic status—the Bellefaire children belonged to a lower social class than the B'nai B'rith group. Most of the Bellefaire families lived in rented apartments, and the majority of fathers were clerks, kindred workers, salesmen, skilled workers, foremen, and semiskilled and unskilled workers.[5] The B'nai B'rith fathers, on the other hand, were mostly professional persons, proprietors, managers, and owners of small businesses.

Since the fathers in both groups resembled each other closely with respect to education, the question arose as to whether the occupational differences were real in relation to subjective social class measures, such as values, mobility aspirations, and stress on education. Thus, although we were not concerned with establishing a cause-and-effect relationship regarding the characteristics of parents that necessitate placement of their children in a treatment institution, we nevertheless came upon important statistical data that support clinical experiences. It seems that the fathers of Bellefaire children were men with weak personalities who, in spite of having as high an educational level as the B'nai B'rith fathers, were not able to achieve as good an occupational status. In addition, the Bellefaire fathers tended to choose wives whose level of education was higher than their own, whereas the B'nai B'rith fathers tended to have a higher educational level than their wives. Our findings also indicate that there is a pattern of interaction between parents (submissive father, domineering mother) that might bring about or influence certain neurotic illnesses in their children that could eventually lead to their placement in a residential treatment center.

The fact that the Bellefaire children were less well informed than the B'nai B'rith children about simple demographic variables concerning their parents deserves further study. Although we do not know what is cause and what is effect—whether the children did not want to be told or whether the parents did not communicate with their children —we think that our examination of communication pattern between parents and children might provide us with important diagnostic clues concerning parent-child relationship.

Verbal Accessibility of the Person

Our hypothesis that adolescents in residential care are less verbally accessible than those living at home was only partially supported. There were no differences between the girls residing at home and those in residential care. The boys at Bellefaire, however, were less verbally accessible than the boys living at home. But why our hypothesis proved true only for boys we do not know. Perhaps the sick boy has to hold on to his concept of masculinity by not verbalizing important attitudes. Or maybe his illness is a result of his verbal inaccessibility. If the latter is true, why is it not also true for girls? Are these differences in verbal accessibility attributable to sex? Although we hypothesized that adolescent boys would be less verbally accessible than adolescent girls, we found this to be true only for the boys at Bellefaire. Thus, while further investigation is needed to throw light on these important questions, we can at this time discuss some of the implications our findings have for the treatment of adolescent boys.

The low accessibility of adolescent boys seems to call for modification of the interview situation. There is question whether the clinical interview, which is based on the ability to talk about important feelings, is really the best method to use with a boy who is not verbally accessible. Further analysis and experimentation should be carried out in this area in order to find better and more efficient ways to help boys in treatment. Until such ways are found, it might be helpful if the worker were aware that the low verbal accessibility of the sick boy is a rather stable characteristic of the individual and that it is the norm of the group rather than a sign of resistance.

Verbal Accessibility of Attitudes

As pointed out, we considered attitudes as being graded on a continuum from determinant, important to dependent, less important; and we selected for study four areas in which determinant attitudes of varying degrees might exist: (1) sexual identity, (2) dependence-independence, (3) parental adequacy, and (4) peer status. Among the adolescents we found group norms concerning the attitudes that are considered important. In other words, the adolescent has a conscious recognition and awareness of the attitudes and feelings he considers important. These adolescent norms of determinant attitudes are recognized not only by the adolescents who are in residential treatment, but also by those who live with their own parents. We did find, however, that the norms of the attitudes that are considered important have a stronger influence on the B'nai B'rith children than on the Bellefaire children.

This became clear when we tested the verbal accessibility of the determinant attitudes. Although both groups showed that there are not only norms with regard to what feelings are considered important, but also group norms as to which feelings are expressed, the consistency among the Bellefaire children was less than the consistency among the B'nai B'rith children. In other words, although the agreement between the two groups signifies that the attitudes the sick child expresses are also influenced by the general culture, this influence is a much weaker one. Superimposed on the cultural norm is the individual problem, which can outweigh the adolescent norm.

It seems to us that these differences in the strength of the norm have implications for treatment. Whereas these norms of important attitudes and the norms of their accessibility are important in working with normal children they have only limited value in working with children who need residential care. Thus, although one would be on relatively safe ground with normal children in assessing the importance of various attitudes and their accessibility in relation to the group norm, one is faced with important differences based on the child's individual problems when this assessment is applied to disturbed children.

Such a situation emphasizes the well-known clinical requirement of being familiar with the child's case history. Only then can we have some insight into what reactions these attitudes might provoke. Even then, the meaning might be so highly individualized and eccentric that no prediction of the child's willingness to discuss his feelings is possible. This, then, partially explains the difficulties one encounters in the interview situation—namely, the element of surprise because of the inability to predict the reaction of the client.

Another important element in treatment about which little is known is the question of whether that which the adolescent recognizes as important coincides with what adults consider important. When we tested the question as to what attitudes are considered as important by adolescents, caseworkers, and cottage staff, we found some agreement between the Bellefaire children and the Bellefaire staff, and between the caseworkers and the cottage staff. But the low agreement among these three groups made it quite obvious that we were dealing with three levels of judgment, or sophistication, in these areas. In other words, we can expect from the adolescent in treatment a different point of view of what attitude he considers determinant. We assume that this is the outcome of our clients' defense mechanisms, but it is well to keep in mind that we found a higher agreement on determinance of attitudes between the girls and their caseworkers than between the boys and their caseworkers. Whether the low agreement between the boys and their caseworkers is the result of the boys' low verbal accessibility or of a different or stronger use of their defense mechanisms, or both, is, however, something we do not know.

Communication Patterns with Different Target Persons

In setting up our hypothesis "that the adolescent will communicate differentially with different target persons," we were guided by our thinking that verbal communication is influenced by the functional role the target persons fulfill or are perceived to fulfill. Furthermore, people tend to differentiate more strongly in regard to the communication of determinant attitudes than they do with dependent attitudes.

When we compared the groups in their overall volume of talking, we found that the mother ranked highest as the recipient of communication in all four groups, even though there is a difference in how much the children talked to her. The B'nai B'rith children communicated proportionately more with their mothers than did the Bellefaire children. As recipient of communication, the fathers of Bellefaire boys ranked nearly as high as the mothers, whereas the B'nai B'rith boys' fathers ranked second to the mothers.

It is interesting to note the girls' communication pattern with respect to their fathers. Although the fathers ranked third in both groups, the B'nai B'rith girls communicated less with their fathers than did the Bellefaire girls.

This differentiation as to what is communicated to different target persons was true not only in regard to the overall amount of talking, but also in the highly determinant and highly unpleasant attitudes that were made accessible to different target persons. We found that, as targets of communication of highly important and highly unpleasant feelings, the boys had a high preference for their parents over their most trusted peer friends. This finding deserves further study, and we think that the general opinion of the profession that the adolescent boy turns away from his parents and seeks support from his peers is not justified. It seems that even though a boy may verbalize his rebellion against his parents, and even oppose them, they are still more important to him, and he is more accessible to them than he is to his peers. Whether this is the result of his struggle to take on adult standards and to find a place in the adult community, or whether his accessibility to his parents is a sign that his real rebellion against his parents took place in late latency or prepuberty, we cannot say with assurance. Yet we are inclined to think that his voiced depreciation of his parents is not as real as he wants to believe or to make us believe. It seems more a case of protesting too much, which he needs to do to bolster his ego.

Since our study pointed to a lack of agreement among the girls themselves with regard to peer status and which attitudes are considered determinant, it is difficult to generalize about the meaning of peer relationships in the life of the girls. This finding, too, seems to indicate that there is more variability in girls in their attitudes toward peers than there is in boys.

A comparison of the communication pattern between boys and girls showed clearly that the role of the "best girl friend" for the girls is more important than the role of the "best boy friend" is for the boys. According to our data, the best girl friend role is very special and, for purposes of communication, comparable to the role of the mother. We hope that further research will tell us whether it is the individual peer friend in the girl's life, as opposed to the peer group in the boy's life, that plays the important role. We are inclined to think that the boy needs his peer group for consensual validation of his opinions, whereas the girl, because of her differential communication pattern, makes use of a peer friend for this purpose.

Our findings that the role of the peer group for the girl is different from that of the boy are supported by another piece of our research. When asked what attitudes they consider to be important in the area of peer relationship, the girls' caseworkers did not agree among themselves. Thus, in this respect, it seems that the caseworkers' thinking is highly individualistic and that they do not use a common base of reference in this area. My own clinical experience in the adolescent girls' cottage at Bellefaire leads me to believe that adolescent girls tend not to group themselves, but prefer friendship with one other girl; at the most they will form small cliques. It was always a major task to bring about an activity that included the whole group, and if such an activity was successful, it never lasted long. This was in contrast to group activities in the boys' cottages. Other people in the field have reported similar experiences and have also pointed out the lack of loyalty of the adolescent girl, e.g., to a club group, which is contrary to the boys' loyalty under similar circumstances.

Should our findings be confirmed, we would have to do some rethinking about our use of the group for girls in the treatment setting. Perhaps we have tried to model adolescent girls' groups after adolescent boys' groups, forgetting that there are differences between these two groups and that we cannot simply pattern one after the other.

Summary

This exploratory field study made a number of comparisons between Jewish adolescent boys and girls who are in treatment in the residential treatment center at Bellefaire and Jewish adolescent boys and girls who live with their parents in the community. We found support for a general hypothesis that the family pattern of the disturbed children differs from that of the normal children.

Our study also pointed out that the adolescent boys under treatment at the center are considerably less verbally accessible than the boys who reside at home. Thus, the low verbal accessibility of the disturbed adolescent boys calls for modification in a treatment situation that is based mainly on the clinical interview.

Both groups of children were well aware of what they communicated to whom. The communication pattern of the children and the importance of the mother as the recipient of communication indicate that the adolescent continues to rely on her as confidant, even though the peer group norm is not to let the parent know this.

Finally, a comparison of the communication pattern between boys and girls showed that the adolescent girls relate much less to the group than do adolescent boys. Since our work with girls in a residential treatment center is based on the same assumption as our work with boys, our findings raise serious questions as to the demand of group living for adolescent girls and suggest rethinking and rearrangement in such areas of daily living as the size of groups and the number of girls per room.

In conclusion, I want to point out that this study was done with a Jewish population and that a replication of it with a non-Jewish population might give different results.

Notes and References

1. See Norman A. Polansky and Erwin S. Weiss, "Determinants of Accessibility to Treatment in a Children's Institution," Journal of Jewish Communal Service, XXXVI (1959), 130-137; Norman A. Polansky, Erwin S. Weiss, and Arthur Blum, "Children's Verbal Accessibility as a Function of Content and Personality," American Journal of Orthopsychiatry, XXXI (1961), 153-169; and Arthur Blum and Norman A. Polansky, "Effect of Staff Role on Children's Verbal Accessibility," Social Work, No. 1 (1961), 29-37.

2. For a more complete presentation of this material, see Esther Appelberg, Verbal Accessibility of Adolescents: A Comparison of Adolescents Living in a Treatment Institution and Adolescents Living in the Community with Their Parents, unpublished doctoral dissertation (Cleveland: Western Reserve University School of Applied Social Sciences, 1961).

3. Our findings recapitulate and support the findings of the earlier work done at Bellefaire. See Blum and Polansky, op. cit.; and Polansky and Weiss, op. cit.

4. From previous research at Bellefaire, certain characteristics of the Bellefaire population were known. Thus, it was possible to select B'nai B'rith club groups that were comparable to the known Bellefaire population. In order to compare the two groups and in order to validate their similarities, the following demographic variables were chosen: (a) place of birth of parents, (b) home ownership, (c) occupation of fathers, and (d) education of children's parents.

5. Using the data from the 16th census of the United States, 1940 [see Occupation Statistics for the United States, 1890-1943 (Washington, D.C.: U.S. Government Printing Office, 1943)], Dr. A. E. Edwards classified occupations. An adaptation of this classification was used as the basis for categorizing the fathers into two groups.

The Cottage meeting as a Therapeutic Tool

In recent years the institutional field—especially in the area of group work practice—has developed a growing awareness and concern about the group living program in residential treatment centers for children. Institutions have found that although the cottage system provides structure helpful in forming a group, structure in itself does not transform the cottage residents into a cohesive group. Application of the social group work method to the group living situation is still a relatively new and experimental development in residential treatment centers for children. It varies in its emphasis on therapeutic discussion groups and recreational activity according to the belief of the individual group worker or the philosophy of the center.[1] Furthermore, our knowledge of the function of the group worker in the cottage group and his role in the group process of everyday living is still limited.

This paper discusses the use made by the unit supervisor of cottage meetings with a group of emotionally disturbed girls as a medium for group development and group functioning in their own behalf. It comments on the girls' inability to use informal activity groups as a source for their own improved social functioning and highlights the theoreti-

Reprinted with permission of the National Association of Social Workers, from Group Work as Part of Residential Treatment (New York, 1965), pp. 142-154.

cal base for the failure of recreational activities in the cottage as a medium for group development.

Setting and Group Composition

Bellefaire Residential Treatment Center has had cottage living arrangements for emotionally disturbed children since 1929. The function of the institution has been defined as follows:

> Bellefaire offers help to children of school age who need individual treatment, skilled personal guidance, and a constructive, planned group living experience. A permissive and non-demanding atmosphere is established in order to help the children cope successfully with problems of personality and behavior which interfere with their ability to achieve satisfying human relationships.[2]

At the time of the events described, the cottage was staffed with three full-time and two relief counselors. The unit supervisor's job was basically administrative and was designed to decentralize the institution into smaller units. It enhanced the work of the cottage counselors and permitted ego-building work with the individual child through manipulation and utilization of his daily life experience.

The decision to have the unit supervisor chair the cottage meeting was based on the assumption that, although his office was in the cottage, he was not involved as intimately in the problems of everyday living as were the counselors who interacted closely with the children. This detachment enabled the unit supervisor to maintain perspective toward the unavoidable pressures and tensions of the girls' everyday life. It gave him the opportunity to keep close to the children, aside from his individual contact, and to observe and participate in the interaction among the children and between the children and staff. There were positive aspects for the girls in having the unit supervisor serve as the leader of the cottage meeting: he was the authority figure best acquainted with their routine, administratively he was nearest the top, and he could support necessary changes. This meant that "passing the buck" could be avoided. (As a rule, the unit supervisor, because of his professional education, has the skill and competence to handle group situations.)

The cottage consisted of 14 adolescent girls ranging in age from 11½ to 17½. The length of stay varied from 4 months to 6 years and 5 months. There was little common ground among the girls. They differed widely in intelligence, emotional and physical development, problems, ego strengths, symptoms, education, learning abilities, social adaptability, and interests. All were in casework treatment. Most of them had entered the institution against their will and came with little understanding of the purposes of the center and why they were placed there. There were some common denominators: the girls' self-esteem was affected; they were all subject, to a greater or lesser degree, to the trauma of separation from their parents; all had been looked on as "deviates" and "misfits" in their previous surroundings. Being in a place with other "misfits" and "deviates" was for them, consciously or unconsciously, the final verdict and reaffirmation of the judgment of their parents, peers, schools, neighbors, and society in general.

The demands of living in a group in the cottage—four or five sharing one bedroom and 14 sharing a bathroom—created problems that had to be resolved in such a way as to give meaning to their group living experience. This in turn would eventually develop in the individual the feeling of being a member of a cohesive group. In other words, a "negative" situation had to be converted into a "positive" condition so that a necessity could be used with positive effect within the overall therapeutic plan. The loss of individuality and privacy would be overcome through participation in one's own daily living arrangements, through meaningful opportunities to express feelings about these arrangements, and through subsequent actions that would return some initiative to the girls, thus effecting change through cooperative activity in limited areas of their cottage situation. It has been noted that changes in one dimension of group life involve changes in another dimension as well.

Content of Cottage Meetings

The cottage meetings were held once a week on a fixed day and hour. Regularity was important in order to provide structure for communication among the girls and between the girls and staff. Prior to the meetings, the unit supervisor discussed the agenda with the rest of the staff. The girls were encouraged to raise any issue that affected their living together, as well as their complaints about staff.

As the group meetings became more meaningful to the girls, events of the week became more accessible to discussion. The girls themselves, as well as the unit supervisor, took the opportunity to direct to the cottage meeting complaints and suggestions that had been aired during the week.

It was decided to handle the problems on a reality basis. The sessions were therapeutic with an educational orientation. Helping the girls focus on reality situations would enable them to cope with their relationships to each other and to the center and would facilitate acquisition of new patterns of behavior. However, the gains that would accrue to the individual or the group from the insights fostered through group interaction were not underestimated. Thus, the girls would be helped to learn to live with one another by participating actively in the solution of problems resulting from living together. This would also give them an opportunity to express their negative feelings toward adult authority and the setting that controlled them. The advantage was that they would do it in the open, as a group with a person in authority present. The goal was clearly an educational one in which cottage situations and experiences were used in such a way that the group would learn from them by going through a corrective emotional experience. Staff wanted to aim at those areas of the ego that were relatively intact and free from conflict, as well as those areas of the self that affected the girls' interaction with each other and with the staff. In short, the educational goal was to correct the social self without focusing on the pathology of any one individual or the specific meaning the symptom had for the individual. (It is well to remember here that all the children were in casework treatment. This is referred to again later.)

Use of complaints about food. As in most institutions, one of the major complaints at Bellefaire was about food. While such complaints were symptomatic of the girls' feelings about the institution in general and while their meaning went deeper than food per se, there was always some reality basis. The complaint about food united the girls. It continued to be important for many meetings and helped them to express their hostility toward one another, staff, and the center in general.

Proposals for change ran wild. When the unit supervisor brought a copy of the menu to one meeting the girls at first showed the same display of temper as at previous meetings. Later, however, they made realistic proposals, as a result of staff efforts to direct to the cottage meeting suggestions that were made over the dinner table during the week and that could be utilized to make some changes in the menu.

The interaction of the girls and their differences of opinion were used to help them experience the process and outcome of group deliberation, which require not only assertion of self but also resolution of conflict. Everyone had to give a little if change were really desired. It was impossible to cook *à la carte*. At the same time, in order not to create an image of an all-powerful leader, the unit supervisor was careful to explain that although suggestions could be made within reasonable limits, these suggestions would have to be discussed with administration. Nevertheless, there was a better chance of influencing preparation of the meals if the group would arrive at a consensus as to what it desired. The unit supervisor volunteered to discuss the proposals with the dietician. Two of the girls for whom food and eating were highly important took it upon themselves to work out a menu and discuss the changes with a staff member and the cook.

The discussion about food was of interest to every girl, allowed the airing of pent-up hostility, and served as a catharsis. Yet, by avoiding interpretation of their complaints, staff controlled the outburst of deeply charged material and helped to repress the girls' dependency feelings and longings for their mothers. Focusing on the reality situation and on what the girls themselves could do with the help of the worker (the unit supervisor) created the conditions for considering action. The action taken as an outcome of these discussions mobilized the girls as a group to look for a solution acceptable to all. By trying to change kitchen policy, the worker conveyed to the girls that he was concerned about their welfare and willing to go to bat for them if they could arrive at a consensus. Thus, these meeings brought about some change in their feelings toward the worker and the center and created the positive feelings necessary for progress. At the same time, just as the worker avoided interpretations of the meaning of their asking for food, he avoided interpretations of the transference feelings toward the worker, staff and the other members of the group.

Small changes became successes and complaints about food became less emotionally charged. While they never disappeared entirely, they lost their importance. It was fascinating to note that while the food did not really change so much and while it disappeared as a symptom of dissatisfaction, no other symptom appeared to take its place. Slowly a new atmosphere developed at the cottage meeting. It was no longer an imposition from the outside, a forum in which to express hostility and negative feeling, but a forum where the girls could look at what was happening to them in their everyday life in the cottage. As they became unified into a cohesive group and shared common problems, some energy was freed so that they could look at their interaction in the living situation. They had reached a point at which it was possible to discuss their interaction and to arrive at a consensus on changes necessary to make life more pleasant.

Development of group identification. While the girls developed some identification as a group, subgroups and cliques continued to exist. The worker frequently had to prevent a clique from taking over the meeting or help cliques to develop identification with the group as a whole and also protect members from being used as scapegoats. At other times, the worker had to help the group express its resentment against a subgroup or help the girls look at what was going on in their interaction so that they could think about better ways to deal with one another. Occasionally, the worker had to help the group exert pressure on individual girls to enable them to acquire certain minimum standards of hygiene and social amenities. Discussion about order and cleanliness in the cottage served this purpose. Repetition of the same accusations and complaints showed the girls that there were certain aspects of their living situation in which an adult could give them little protection and that changes depended on each one of them.

By avoiding deeper interpretation of their behavior and, at the same time, by putting demands on them, staff made it difficult for the girls to use glib excuses for their behavior. Many of these girls were rather sophisticated, especially in the area of treatment. Most had been in treatment before coming to the institution and all were now in individual treatment. Thus, most of the girls had what can be called a "sophistication in treatment," "great insight," and quite a treatment vocabulary. If staff had let them explore and discuss the reasons for their own and each other's habits, comments would have arisen such as, "I don't know how to take care of myself because my mother never wanted me to grow up," or "She leaves the place a mess because she thinks she still has to fight her mother." Instead, the girls moved from accusing one another to helping the weaker ones and to paying closer attention to their own habits. They developed a feeling that the bathroom was not Bellefaire's or the staff's but their own.

Protection of individuals. Another illustration emphasizes the sense of belonging and the group feeling the girls had developed. It highlights the point made previously, that often it is the task of the worker to protect an individual member so that she does not become an outcast. Not infrequently during such discussions the worker had to take an active role and intervene to protect a girl, while at the same time allowing some group pressures to exist.

> N, a 15-year-old girl who had revealed herself as a soiler, aroused a great deal of rejection and hostility from the group, as she denied her soiling and did not change her clothes when she had an accident. This, of course, was the way she expressed her hostility toward the others, as if she wanted "to stink everybody out." In addition, she was a tattler and played mean tricks on the girls. While the girls were disturbed by these qualities, they were more worried about N's soiling because they feared that this hurt their cottage reputation. N and the girls bickered, and each day a delegation came to complain about N and demand her removal from the cottage. N, too, complained about the girls. One day she came to the worker in tears after learning the girls wanted to gang up on her and wash her with a commercial cleansing powder. At this point, the worker felt that the whole matter had to be discussed in a cottage meeting. This was suggested to the group and N was prepared for it.
>
> Nearly everyone had something to say in the meeting, most of which was hostile. N sat crossly and did not say a word. When the worker thought enough hostility had been expressed, he intervened by bringing the discussion around

to the question of why the girls were at Bellefaire. Thus, the girls were helped to see that each of them had a reason for being in the center, that while not all of them had such a disturbing symptom, each had some kind of problem that also made her difficult to live with. This motivated some of the group to look at themselves and to think and talk about how others had ganged up on them and made life difficult for them. At the same time, while the other girls rediscovered the fact that they, like N, had a reason for being at the center, N was helped to see that the group had a right to protect its welfare and to expect elementary hygienic habits from her; that while at this point she could do nothing to stop her soiling, she could clean herself whenever she had an accident.

It was hard to get through to N, who had little feeling of shame, little motivation to change, and much hostility. The recommendation to take more responsibility did not stop her from soiling, but she started to pay attention to her personal hygiene. Thus, while the symptom did not disappear, N handled herself differently. This also brought a change in the group's attitude toward her. N gained some satisfaction from the discussion, in which the others had to face some of their own difficulties; perhaps most important for N at her stage of development was the protection she received from the worker, who did not let the group harm her. Thus N could begin, through the worker, to relate to the group.

Preparation for change in group membership. Cottage meetings were also used to prepare the girls for the arrival or departure of members. This is a necessary function, for although the groups in a treatment center are relatively stable, they are not fixed or closed and changes do take place as new members are admitted and old ones leave. Preparation helps the group to maintain its cohesiveness, at the same time making it flexible enough to absorb a new member by extending itself as a group to the newcomer, or to feel less threatened by the loss of a member. These discussions helped many to recall their own feelings around placement and their first day in the institution. While this served as a catalytic agent, staff kept the educational aim in mind and helped the girls focus on what had made it difficult or easy to find their place in the cottage. Discussion of "going and coming" also helped the girls feel a sense of participation. They were helping one of their group to leave for her own good and they were helping another enter their midst.

Focusing on a common goal through active participation in the absorption of a new girl helped strengthen the in-feeling of the group as well as their sense of belonging to the center. Admission became an issue and concern not only for the staff but for the whole cottage group. Participation is especially important in a setting where members have no say about admissions, and the new member can all too easily be used as a target for expressions of hostility toward administration. Each additional member takes away some living space the old-timers have become used to regarding as their own, such as an empty closet or drawer.

Values resulting from meetings. The material presented so far points to the fact that the cottage meeting was helpful in changing an administrative unit and physical group into a group of girls who acquired a positive feeling for each other and a sense of having a common purpose in being at the center. The physical setup of the cottage gained importance for them—it became *their* cottage; they cared how it looked to others and what others thought of them, and considered how they could be more comfortable in their living situation. This was achieved by discussing problems as they arose out of group experience within the context of everyday living. Although the sessions were educational in their goal, the content—the concern with basic aspects of living like eating, sleeping, cleanliness, and so on—provided a rich and meaningful experience and created the possibility of forming new relationships with other members of the group on the basis of sharing fundamental human experiences. Free to express their anger, hurt, and frustrations in a controlled setting, they could redirect their energy into new channels of interacting and relating with each other. This was done with the active participation of the worker, who focused the discussion and intervened in such a way that the meeting would be more than a "gripe session" or a forum for free-floating feelings.

The process of the discussion method helped the girls not only to express what they felt, but to learn that they could talk instead of acting out. It helped them to learn to listen to each other. This, too, carried over in their everyday living. They learned that as a group they had meaning and the power to achieve goals and that in this respect they resembled the adults around them. Adult authority was no longer something undependable, unreasonable, hostile, distributing and withholding without reason. It was an authority that could be challenged and questioned. Although this authority encouraged their participation, there was a limit to this participation and to their power of decision. They learned to understand the painful fact that Bellefaire was a treatment center in which they had been placed for reason of illness and it was not in their power to make some decisions; Bellefaire was helping them to prepare for making decisions. By acting as a group, they (who had never really belonged to any group and never had feelings of participation or belonging) were provided with an educational experience that was really a re-education; they learned to live with and get along with others and to acquire new habit values and new standards. The fact that the worker invited their participation and the resultant positive feelings toward the accepting adult encouraged the girls to want to take on adult standards.

Problems of Institutionalization

If we talk about group living experiences, it is precisely the area discussed above—the day-to-day life in the cottage—that lends itself to skillful use by the group worker and the group work method.[3] There is hardly a child in an institution who has not been in conflict with his mother from early childhood. This conflict has expressed itself in eating disturbances, sleeping disturbances, cleanliness and so on. It is in this manner that the child, in his pre-Oedipal development, expresses his sexual and hostile impulses toward his parents. Because of his disturbed relationship to his parents and his lack of identification with them, he cannot take on adult standards. In the institution he carries on this struggle with the parent substitutes in precisely the same areas in which he fought his parents. Emotional development in the pre-Oedipal phase does not keep pace with biological development. Adolescence reawakens and strengthens infantile feelings and drives and makes for an increase in asocial attitudes. Regression is not only the result of being adolescent; it can also result from being in a group institution. Contagion in the group situation can weaken individual control. Thus, it is precisely in the living situation where the group worker has the responsibility and the chance to provide a new positive human experience around the basic human needs.

Handling of transference. Transference in the institution is a complicated problem. With whom does the child enter into a transference relationship in this setting? Is it his caseworker, his cottage counselor, his teacher, his unit worker? Although we might hope to structure the institutional setting in such a way that the child will divert his transference feelings toward the person whom we see as desirable and who can handle the transference—i.e., the caseworker—in reality the child often will not follow our structure and will select his own target.

We shall not attempt here to enter this theoretical discussion. This would be beyond the scope of this paper, and has been discussed in great detail elsewhere.[4] We point out that transference can take place also outside the clinical interview. In the group situation transference elements are present in the relationship among the children and between the children and staff. At Bellefaire staff were aware of these factors and used them to understand the group, but did not interpret them. Focus was on the reality situation; staff tried to undo old habits and help the children learn new ones.

In this institution the transference was handled in the casework situation. Collaboration between the unit supervisor and the caseworker was very full; there was a constant flow of information between them. Furthermore, children were helped by cottage staff to express to the caseworker individual problems that the cottage meeting stimulated. Similarly, the caseworker encouraged the girls to bring problems in connection with group living to the cottage meeting.

Failure of group activities. The cottage meeting also became the forum for planning recreational activities—parties, sports, ceremonies and the like. These informal activities were an outlet for the individual girl, but did little to create cohesiveness in the group. The population was too diversified in range of intelligence and interest. The girls were more interested in sunning themselves if the weather were nice, going out with boys, or just being idle. They preferred to spend leisure time on their own or with an individual girl friend. Except for rare occasions, group activities in the cottage were not to their taste. This continued to be true despite the fact that some of the recreational activities sponsored by the cottage were successful and enjoyed by the girls.

At each cottage meeting staff had to struggle anew to involve the girls in planning the recreational activities. Then there was a real struggle to help the group follow through with the plan on which they had just decided. This experience reflected an essential difference between girls' and boys' groups: the girls were less interested in group activity, were inclined to be less active than the boys, and were not as interested in activities that involved only their own sex.

The differences in group behavior of boys and girls were further borne out in a research study that compared Bellefaire residents with a control group living with their families.[5] One of the findings of this study was that there are major differences between boys and girls as to how they relate to and use groups. The girls were found to prefer an individual "best girl friend," the boys group involvement.

The study also showed much greater individual differences among girls than among boys. Boys and girls were given a set of scales in the form of sentences in which attitudes were present. The attitudes were in the four basic areas of concern to adolescents: (1) sexual identity, (2) dependence-independence, (3) parental adequacy, and (4) peer relationship. They were first asked to rank these items in order of importance and then as to the feelings of pleasantness-unpleasantness. On both scales agreement was found among the boys as a group and the girls as a group as to which attitudes they considered important and which they considered unpleasant. Yet the agreement among the boys as a group was greater than among the girls. In other words, in these two areas the girls showed much greater individual differences than the boys. Greater individual differences were also found among the girls as a group when the attitudes communicated were analyzed. Although the boys as well as the girls were influenced by the group norms as to what they communicated, the influence of these group norms was weaker in the girls' group than it was in the boys' group.

The preference of a best girl friend might explain the unwillingness of the girls at Bellefaire to engage in recreational activities as a group. Being with a girl friend is of greater importance than spending free time with a group of girls.[6] The finding of greater individual differences among girls than among boys raises the question whether the adolescent girl is more complex or individualistic than the adolescent boy. If the girls are inclined to be more individualistic than boys, this might explain the difficulties staff had in bringing the Bellefaire girls together for recreational activities as a group.[7] The finding that the girls prefer their best girl friend is consistent with their unwillingness to do things as a group. These factors that indicate greater individuality among girls than boys raise a number of questions for the future of the cottage setting. Since there is less community of interest among adolescent girls, would it not be beneficial to provide more privacy than has been available previously and to take into account in the physical setting the importance of the girl friend and of the one-to-one relationship?

Recommendations

The writer recommends building cottages to accommodate one or two in a room instead of four and five. Social workers have to be much more creative, daring, and individualistic in their approach toward the individual girl. Less stress should be placed on involving girls in cottagewide recreational activities, and allowances should be made to foster expression of individual ability and interest. The small clique should not be opposed, but should be used as the nucleus for group living. Instead of working in the recreational area with the whole cottage, a skilled group worker can involve small groups and work with them either as discussion or recreational groups, depending on the group itself. In the adolescent girls' cottage, staff worked successfully with a group of four who showed a common interest in music and travel and who felt the need for discussion on a more sophisticated basis than others in the cottage did. At the outset it was feared that this might become a status group, and to offset this the whole cottage was invited to participate in the activities of this quartet from time to time. For example, they were asked to attend an "Israeli Night" at which the main attraction was Israeli food. On another occasion, a slide lecture on Mexico (with Mexican food served) was arranged for the whole cottage. It soon became evident that the other girls were neither interested nor jealous and the quartet continued its activities. Some of the other girls found satisfaction in sports on a regular basis with one of the counselors when they realized that the quartet's activities were too "highbrow" for them. A number of girls showed an interest in the theater and worked on campus to earn money for tickets to performances they wanted to attend. Again, this was an activity that had only limited appeal and was confined to those genuinely interested without detriment to the group as a whole. Of course, as time went on more and more girls became interested in one activity or another as word got around. The group worker can utilize these small units for the benefit of the whole cottage. Assistance to informal small-group activities seems consistent with the study's finding of the close relationship girls have to one of their peers and to the weak influence of group norms on them.

In cottage meetings, the girls were able to take on a group activity with the cottage as a whole because it was vital to their day-to-day functioning and pertinent to their individual needs. This much of their individuality they had to give up, but no more. This readiness can be utilized by the same group worker who assists the small group to involve the whole cottage group in connection with the everyday problems as they arise in the cottage.

Experience has indicated that there is a variety of individual differences that must be catered to individually or through small groups within the cottage, but there are enough areas of concern to foster group spirit and to build the ego of the individual girl. These are the areas of every day living-together, using the same facilities, receiving newcomers, and separating them from old-timers. In short, these are the areas of basic human needs that allow the girls to find newer and more positive ways of interacting with each other and with the adult in charge.

Notes and References

1. John Matsushima, "Group Work with Emotionally Disturbed Children in Residential Treatment," Social Work, Vol. 7, No. 2 (April 1962), pp. 62-70.
2. "Catalogue of Services" (Cleveland, Ohio: Bellefaire Residential Treatment Center, 1958), p. 2. (Mimeographed.)

3. Elliot Studt, "Therapeutic Factors in Group Living," Child Welfare, Vol. 35, No. 1 (January 1956).

4. See M. F. Mayer, "The Parental Figures in Residential Treatment," Social Service Review, Vol. 34, No. 3 (September 1960), pp. 273-285.

5. Esther Appelberg, "Verbal Accessibility of Adolescents; A Comparison of Adolescents Living in a Treatment Institution and Adolescents Living in the Community With Their Parents." Unpublished doctoral dissertation, School of Applied Social Sciences, Western Reserve University, Cleveland, Ohio, 1961.

6. Helen Deutsch, The Psychology of Women: A Psychoanalytic Interpretation (New York: Grune and Stratton, 1944). Observations made by workers in group-serving agencies point also to the lack of loyalty of the adolescent girl (e.g., to a club group), which is contrary to boys' loyalty.

7. When staff asked the girls and the Bellefaire caseworkers and cottage counselors to rank in importance the items that presented attitudes in the area of peer relationship, little consensus was found. All differed as to which attitudes they considered important. This implies not only that the girls view peer relationship from an individualistic point of view and are not unified as to the meaning this relationship has for them, but that the caseworkers are not unified in their professional body of knowledge in this area. The same holds true for the cottage counselors, who have occasion to observe this area closely day by day. In short, the area of peer relationship not only seems to have different meaning for different girls, but is an area in which professionals use their individual judgment rather than a judgment that has grown out of a common body of knowledge.

A Progress Report on the Ongoing Foster Parent Workshop

The Institute on Foster Parenthood had its start with an invitation extended by Yeshiva University to 12 foster care agencies in New York City. In this meeting, which was attended by executive staff and supervisors, there was exploration of the need for education of foster parents that would concern foster parenthood, caseworkers, and supervisors, and which would be under the sponsorship of the University.

Planning Committee

All agencies' representatives present expressed the need for and desirability of such an undertaking, and a Planning Committee from the represented agencies was formed.[1]

Federation of Protestant Welfare Agencies

The committee expressed the hope that the impartial educational climate of a university setting would enable foster parents to engage in active listening and to participate in free discussion. Such an insti-

---

Published originally in CHILD WELFARE, XLVII, 2, February 1968.

tute should raise the status of foster parents in the community, since it gives recognition to the contribution foster parents are making to the nation's children. This recognition can be used for recruitment purposes.

The committee pointed out that New York City has 30 agencies with foster care programs serving 11,000 foster children. Some of these agencies function together in certain areas of foster home care. They do so under the auspices of the Family and Child Welfare Division of the Community Council of Greater New York. Many of these agencies have their own programs for foster parents, some of which are of long duration and others of which are being established now. Most of these programs consist of monthly group meetings of foster parents in each agency.

Programs and Goals

The institute was seen by the committee as a pilot project to test the readiness of agencies to participate in systematic, interagency foster-parent training and to test foster parents' willingness to engage themselves in active learning within the framework of a school of social work that was willing to set up a program to serve the unique needs of foster parents.

It was hoped that through the cooperative effort of Yeshiva University and the New York City public and private agencies caring for 11,000 children we could demonstrate that the role of foster parenthood can be taught and that it is the responsibility of schools of social work and social work agencies to provide the education. Therefore, the courses would concern themselves with child rearing as it is accomplished in the different stages of child development. The courses would include some material on growth and behavior, but the emphasis would be on the special dimension of the foster-parent–child relation, and the particular role of foster parents in respect to the foster child in the home. Our assumptions were that all foster parents are concerned about the special problems of their foster children as such. All foster children come into placement with at least one strike against them, and many foster parents feel that they must go beyond the functions of natural parents in their relations with the child.

The course material is being presented in 15 sessions for the foster parents, who meet one evening a week. The same material was presented in a two-day seminar for supervisors, and a three-day seminar for caseworkers, prior to the beginning of the foster parents' classes.

For the purpose of this institute, we used the definition of the Child Welfare League of America for foster care:

> "Foster family care is [that] which provides substitute family care for a planned period for a child when his own family cannot care for him for a temporary or extended period, and when adoption is neither desirable nor possible." [2]

We decided that our emphasis for this training program would be on child development, and that a special dimension would be added; namely, what it means to be a foster child and what it means to be a foster parent.

The goals of the project were to establish:

Patterns for foster parents' training.
Patterns for caseworkers' training as related to their specific tasks in working with foster parents.
Patterns for training of supervisors who will serve as teachers to their agency staff, to foster parents, and to caseworkers in the field of foster care.

The aim is to develop a series of courses that will be applicable to foster parents, caseworkers, and supervisors. Each of these courses will differ to some extent in its objectives and goals.

Content of the Foster-Parent Course

The courses would concern themselves with child rearing in the different stages of child development, including content on growth and behavior as appropriate. The emphasis would be on the special issues that enter into the foster-parent–child relations. Although the concepts of growth and behavior and the issues in child rearing are universal (such as, for example, Erikson's concept of autonomy versus shame and doubt in the anal period), the course would not be a course in growth and behavior per se, but in helping foster parents to observe, understand, and respond appropriately to such current experiences as the temper tantrum of a 2-year-old as part of normal growth. As the foster parents understand what behavior is likely to accompany particular stages of development, they can function more securely in dealing with both the "natural problems" of children, and with the special variations that may occur because of the child's situation in foster care.

The specific developmental phases selected would depend on the ages of the foster children of the participants. We have identified certain key issues in the developmental phases of the life of foster children, on the basis of which the material is presented. These are such issues as separation, identity, conflict between sets of parents, learning, regression, play, and so forth.

To increase the identification with a formal educational process, the courses would be held at the university. Criteria for selection of foster parents would specify that they have not been with the agency for longer than a year. (Actually we were not able to hold to this first criterion, and had to make modifications.) There would be no educational requirement. The parents would be selected by the agencies, who would pay for their carfare, their evening meals when necessary, and their babysitters. Foster parents would commit themselves to participate regularly in the sessions.

The university and the agencies would establish a feedback system and work out an evaluation plan. The university would issue a certificate to the foster parents who participate in the institute.

The Caseworkers' Course

The course content for caseworkers would be essentially the same as that developed for foster parents. Throughout the placement the caseworker continues to work with the complex triangular relationship of child, parent, and foster parent. The caseworkers, in their three-day seminar, would consider how to apply the course content in their professional role with the foster parent.

Criteria for the selection of caseworkers are that they be selected by their agencies, and that they fulfill the functions of the caseworker in the agency, though they need not hold a master's degree. They would be primarily the workers whose foster-parent clients would attend the institute. Actually we were not able to meet this last criterion either, and a minority of caseworkers have foster-parent couples in the institute.

It is recognized that the variations in professional background make the caseworker group a heterogeneous one, and might perhaps slow down the learning. However, it is also recognized that even persons with a master's degree are not always well-grounded in child development and behavior, and so the course would not necessarily involve repetition but could deepen understanding. Members of the group will learn at different levels, and can contribute to each other.

The Supervisors' Course

The content of the course for supervisors would be the same as that for the foster parents and caseworkers. The objective would be to train supervisors to teach this material to foster parents on an ongoing basis in their respective agencies.

The supervisors would be selected by their agencies, and would have at least a minimum of experience in the supervisory role. They would start their own groups in their agencies upon completion of their training program.

Prior to the foster-parent institute, they would meet for two full working days on agency time. Each supervisor would then be a nonparticipating observer and recorder in three foster-parent sessions. The time spent on these would also be the agency's. At the end of the first semester, the supervisors would meet for another two days to discuss their experiences in the foster-parent sessions, to evaluate them, and to work out guidelines for their own training sessions.

Planning and Reporting

After the proposal was accepted by the U.S. Children's Bureau, the Planning Committee continued to meet in order to work out details of this undertaking. The details included selection of participants, selection of leaders, choice of time, data to be obtained from the agencies and the participants, feedback from school to agencies and vice versa, and publicity. At present the committee is working on methods by which the effectiveness of the workshops can be ascertained.

Operation of the Program

Progress of the program has been as follows: The foster parent-hood institute opened with an orientation meeting for the foster parents. The group leaders and representatives of the Planning Committee were also present, and they were greeted by the regional representative of the Children's Bureau. About 80% of the foster parents came to this meeting and were presented with a kit: a small briefcase containing paper and pencil for future use, a booklet about Yeshiva University, a copy of Spock's *Baby and Child Care,* and several pamphlets published by the Children's Bureau: *Infant Care, Your Child from One to Six, Your Child from Six to Twelve, Home Play and Play Equipment,* and *Accidents and Children.* This kit was provided not as an assignment, but as a resource on which they could draw. As institute director, I explained the goal and format of the foster-parent workshop:

> "We are facing the tremendous task of studying complex human beings. How can we help to make successful lives?
>
> "Knowledge about behavior and its causes is increasing rapidly. We want to give you foster parents some of the results of studies and projects, especially as they relate to the foster child and to the effect of his separation. There is a great deal that we don't know, but we want you to be free to ask questions. In some ways you know more about the children than we do—you see them all day long in natural play, asleep, and in good and bad phases. Though we want to consider all possible questions, we know there are not always 'right' answers—there are only 'right' questions.
>
> "We have kept the groups small to encourage free discussion; no group is over 16 in number. Courses are being given at this time for caseworkers in foster care, and also for supervisors. If a couple of strangers appear at times in the groups, they are merely observers and are to be ignored. At the end of the series we will have a meeting to see if the project has seemed worthwhile, and again we want frank comments. Has it been too much? Too little? Too long? Too short? Profitable? Have questions been answered?"

These remarks were planned to put the participants at ease, and when the meeting was thrown open for questions there were several, all raised by the foster fathers:

"Shall we stay in the same group?"

"It there any thought of visiting others?"

"If we have an infant and a 5-year-old as foster children, why are we assigned to the group that will discuss only the 5-year-old?" (The teachers observed here that they will adjust to the discussion in their groups, not cut it off.)

"Will there be an extension of the groups if we want it?"

At the close of the meeting, most of the group accepted the invitation to inspect the library, where shelves had been specially arranged for our group. Several members took out books or pamphlets.

It is, of course, too early to report on the outcome of these workshops for supervisors, caseworkers, and foster parents, but I can report that the caseworkers' institute did take place, and that 16 caseworkers from 8 agencies participated. The number of participants was larger than we had expected.

There seems to be a consensus that it was too compressed. Yet there also seems to be agreement that the material was valuable, and that it was presented from an unusual and helpful point of view insofar as the focus was actually on the foster parent, based on dynamic understanding of placement from the viewpoint of both child and foster parents.

The supervisors have finished the first part of their seminar. They are now engaged in observing and recording the foster-parent seminars. The class consists of 11 supervisors from 8 agencies. So far attendance has been excellent.

Concluding Comments

We have taken into consideration from session to session that, since foster parents are nonprofessionals actively involved in solving problems of child rearing, supervision, and management, the amount of theoretical material they are willing and able to absorb is limited. Usually they want specific answers to difficulties they encounter in their tasks. Yet we must keep in mind that these meetings are neither group therapy nor problem-solving clinics. Questions in regard to handling children should be considered in relation to their wider implications, with application to the whole group and not just to the individual who raises the question. The aim is to help foster parents develop a more knowledgeable approach to problem-solving, rather than to suggest specific techniques. We hope that foster parents can learn more about children, and that such knowledge can be translated into better coping with problems of caring for foster children. The parents might also become more aware of the community implications of foster care. They might gain more understanding of the child's own parents. It is hoped that they will be able to recognize danger signals and potential problems, and talk freely with the caseworker before a crisis erupts. It is hoped, too, that there will be a closer identification with the professional goals of the agency.

Notes and References

1. The Planning Committee consisted of Lorraine Loustalot, Catholic Charities; Rose Gutman, Bureau of Child Welfare; Annie L. Tucker, Sheltering Arms Children's Service; Everett Coutant, Catholic Home Bureau; Eileen Kinsella, Catholic Charities of Brooklyn; Elizabeth Radinsky, Jewish Child Care Association; James J. Nolan, Angel Guardian Home; and Vernon Daniels, Federation of Protestant Welfare Agencies.
2. Child Welfare League of America Standards for Foster Family Care Service (New York: Child Welfare League of America, 1959), p. 5.

The Case against Records, with Special Emphasis on Children as Persons in Their Own Right

Long before current concerns about privacy, social workers have questioned the fact that case records could be subpoenaed and used against their clients. This paper examines the ethical question of the writing and keeping of records by professional social workers without the informed consent of the person involved, or the latter's opportunity to challenge the data accumulated in these records; and presents a case against keeping records once a client has left an agency.

The professional assumption has been that the record has a purpose as long as the client is in treatment. Richmond introduced systematic recording into social casework, using a model presented by a psychiatrist, Dr. Howe.[1] A quarter of a century later, Hamilton solidified a theory of recording in her classic text.[2] The record was seen as a tool that would make the profession more scientific.

A cursory review of the social casework literature since then reveals that recording itself has hardly ever been challenged except for reasons of cost. A rare exception is an experimental study by Frings, Kratovil and Polemis, published in 1958.[3] Their study seemed not to influence agencies' practices of keeping records, even though some of the results deserved the profession's serious consideration. Some of their conclusions are summarized here: From the caseworker's point of view, the record was written for somebody else. It had value for the record writer mainly because of the necessity to rethink and formulate the case material, but the preponderant use of the record was made by supervisors. The study demonstrated that supervisors "read approximately 20% or less of a caseworker's caseload for the purpose of supervisory conferences in any one month—possibly an additional 10% or 12% of the casework load read for other purposes was also used for supervisory conferences. . . . The majority of case discussions between a supervisor and a caseworker did not involve the use of written material, although it is almost axiomatic in social work that case supervision should ideally be based on the written record. . . . Use of records by administrative and special staff was sporadic—relatively infrequent in relation to the total caseload for special purposes at particular times." The use by other caseworkers was relatively small and mainly in the application process.[4,5,6,7]

The diagnostic and the functional schools differ as to their treatment approach and therefore also as to what should go into the record. Both questioned the ethics involved in keeping records and the contradiction between the promise of confidentiality and an existing file, yet neither seemed to be seriously troubled and both continued to keep files long after the client left the agency. The functional school talked about the importance of the agency record in assuring continuity, assessment and service. The diagnostic school talked about the importance of the psychosocial study, the gathering of facts, diagnosis and treatment plans. Accountability was a concern to both schools, and records were seen as assuring all the foregoing. One could probably make a valid assumption for both schools of thought: "Once a client, always a client; once in need, always in need."

The record was thus considered not only an important tool for ongoing treatment, but a repository should the client or another member of his family return for treatment. The role model was the physician, who had medical data available for annual checkups or future treatment; as the physician and the hospital guard the physical health of their client, so the social worker and the social agency would safeguard the emotional and social health of their client. The social agency seldom questioned seriously whether the client had given him a mandate to keep material about him during treatment or after treatment; neither of the two schools of social work discussed the issue of recording in the initial interview or in the "contract." [8] Yet the question of keeping records is, finally, an ethical one. It is a question of self-determination, privacy, inner and outer freedom, and dignity.

The Client's Right to Consent

As long as records are considered working notes to help the practitioner give better service to the client, a case can be made for them. Beyond that, if records are kept, they are an invasion of privacy and an intrusion into personal rights. If records have to be kept about medical, social or emotional illness, and this material were needed again, who should keep them—the helper or the one who asks for help? If a person has a medical, social, economic or emotional problem, does that mean he is incompetent to keep data about himself?

It seems to me that any law that asks the doctor or the social worker to keep a record once the patient finishes treatment is an anachronism. It is a fossil from the time when the concept of privacy was hazier than it is today. It is a remnant of a paternalistic attitude: people are incompetent; they have to be cared for. The physician, heir of the primitive medicine man, fitted perfectly into the role of guardian. Part of what he guarded and is still guarding is the measure of his own ignorance. Yet the mystery of his real or assumed knowledge about life and death helped invest him with power and magic and increase his own feelings of omnipotence. Probably every man who tries to help people and deals with human misery needs some sense of effectiveness, or, if you will, of omnipotence. The person who asks for help needs to believe in the helper. Thus, although this mutuality of feelings and expectations serves a purpose, the resulting system lends itself to abuse of power.[9,10,11,12]

As someone educated within the Freudian psychological framework, I cannot negate the importance of this framework, and thus the importance of a psychosocial history, longitudinal studies, diagnostic judgments and recording. How much of this is necessary and how it is to be used is another question.

I agree with Erikson's statement: "You may learn about the nature of things and find out what you can do with man, but the true nature of man reveals itself only in the attempt to do something for him." Or, to put it differently, it is the old question whether helping people, be it social work, teaching, psychiatry or medicine, is a science or an art. At present it is both. Research and rigorous thinking are needed to make these professions more scientific, but art will always play a role in our use of knowledge. It is the art of helping people that enables us to use our knowledge creatively.

A client who comes to an agency and asks for service is in an immediate situation. He does not expect the agency to keep records of his secret, his fear, his hope or shame, beyond the termination of service. Unlike us, the client assumes that at a certain point he can do without us and attend to his own needs. His contract with us is not for life.

Do Records Reveal Sufficient Truth to Justify Our Respect for Them?

A diagnosis or an assessment is as good as and as reliable as the facts on which it rests. Whether a mother who retells the early childhood of her child is always a reliable informant, able to recall exactly or without distortion such information as age of weaning or toilet training, is open to question. The human mind has its own method of recall, a selective one, based on denial, repression, pain and pleasure. One can probably assume that, barring unusual circumstances, the worker will get a mixture of fiction and truth. Our concept of psychosocial history is based on the psychoanalytic model. Yet we do not use patient recall as analysts do, nor is our aim the same as theirs.

We exaggerate the meaning of the psychosocial history. It takes more to understand a client than a psychosocial history taken by a psychiatrist, psychologist or social worker. The best papers dealing with clinical evidence are Erikson's "The First Psychoanalyst" and "The Nature of Clinical Evidence." Erikson points to the debt owed to Freud, who gave us "a controversial tool . . . for the detection of that aspect of the total image of man which in a given historical period is being neglected or exploited . . . by the prevailing technology or ideology." Probing deeply into the encounter between the helper and the helped, he stresses the participation of the analyst's self and the kind of evidence introduced by "what a patient said to me, how he behaved in doing so and what I, in turn, thought and did

. . . (which cannot be replaced by) research windows in the form of one-way screens (however legitimate their contribution)." [13] In other words, as each client has his own way of telling his story, the worker has his own way of listening. This listening is conditioned by a frame of reference, degree of intuition, empathy, and capacity to listen. He is critical. Statements such as "he admitted," "he denied," "he agreed," attest to the critical attitude of the worker, and sometimes the client is subtly coerced or manipulated into admitting, agreeing or lying, perhaps to please us or to manipulate us, or to protect his privacy. Who of us could not tell some stories that bear this out?

Observations recorded out of context or as isolated incidents are meaningless—for example, a classic comment selected at random about a 1½-year-old: "He did not communicate"; or the observation about the 13-year-old "who has homosexual tendencies." For someone working within the psychoanalytic framework, it is accepted that all youngsters go through a period of love for the same sex; thus, is it always important to record this? Somebody else who misunderstands the theory or applies another might observe only that "he is homosexual." This can happen within one agency; it certainly happens with different agencies looking at the same record. This probably explains why no agency accepts a client for its own service without making its own study. Rightly or wrongly, one agency does not trust the other.

Tape recordings also have their limitations. "In contrast to the written recording, which represents the experience of the writer as participant, the tape recording represents the added dimension of all who participate in its creation. . . . Increased authenticity rather than objectivity is derived from tape recording." [14]

In the final analysis any written record that represents the experience between two persons or in a group is basically the experience of the person who writes the record. It is how he sees the "truth" at the moment. At its best it is his understanding and his view of another human being.

The Danger of Record Keeping

Social work as a profession has probably never been fully at peace with the practice of keeping records and with such a result as the "Social Service Exchange." Some agencies did not subscribe to that

service. Individual social workers fought it. Teicher argued against it
most eloquently in his paper, "Let's Abolish the Social Service Exchange." [15] Yet today we witness an increasing invasion of privacy,
with misuse and abuse of personal information:

Put a Computer Teletypewriter in Your Office
$70 per month

And get past psychiatric histories for $7 each. You enter
patient's answers on tape and computer history prints out.
Finished copy, immediate return. Get a secret password and
share time with us. Available throughout the United States
and Canada.

The Personality Laboratory
Lutheran General Hospital
Park Ridge, Illinois 60068
(Tel. 312, 696-2210, ext. 1567)

MMPI's and Treatment Evaluation Questionnaires available.[16]

It is a sad commentary upon our ethics that we, who worry about
the invasion of our privacy—possible misuse of social security numbers, and the harm of juvenile and adult court records—venture into
enterprises such as the one described in the ad. We complain about
Big Brother, about discrimination against the poor, yet we are ready
to reinforce and refine the same kind of discrimination in professionally sanctioned journals under the name of science and efficiency
of service. That ad represents private enterprise; the New York Children's Council's effort to computerize information about children
represents private and public agency enterprise. The demand of the
State of New York that names of children in placement be recorded
with the state highlights its encroachment upon the right to privacy
of the poor.

Who if not the poor will be registered with a social agency or mental
health clinic? The computer teletypewriter, like its predecessor, the
"Social Service Exchange," is a logical outcome of the preservation of
records. Once you accumulate, you have to dispense. When you pile
up stock, you have to find a market. Whether one deals with bombs or
personal data, the principle is the same. Information, diagnoses,
assessments, treatment plans, service plans—all seem to hold magic,
since "what is written down must be true." Will collecting data or

passing it on to others and taking it from others give us the magic to eliminate poverty, find adoptive parents, or make peace between a husband and wife?

Agencies have to be accountable to the state; the taxpayer has a right to know how his money is being spent. But consider the scope of what we do: register children's names with the state because the state participates in the cost; keep records once the service is terminated; share information with other public or private agencies, social service exchanges or computer services. In the Supreme Court case of Mrs. Barbara James v. New York State, Justice Marshall cited the fourth amendment in his arguments against making home visits a criterion in determining Aid to Dependent Children eligibility. In his minority opinion, Marshall pointed out "that federal regulations do not require that the worker actually see the child during the home visit. . . . A paternalistic notion that a complaining citizen's constitutional rights can be violated as long as the state is somehow helping him is alien to our nation's philosophy." [17] He could not see the unwanted home visit as anything less than a search; he could not accept the ruling that the state could condition the receipt of welfare benefits upon the waiver of one's constitutional right to privacy in his own home. He also stated:

> Would the majority sanction, in the absence of probable cause, compulsory visits to all American homes for the purpose of discovering child abuse? Or is the court proposal to hold as a matter of constitutional law that a mother, merely because she is poor, is substantially more likely to injure or exploit her children? [18]

Prior to the ruling of the Supreme Court a federal district court ruled that the Department of Social Service could not legally deny assistance to an otherwise eligible person because of the refusal to permit a home visit, a "search" within the terms of the fourth amendment.

My question is: Carrying Marshall's opinion one step further, should there be laws that require that the names of patients who are drug addicts or mentally retarded be forwarded to the state? As we know, child guidance and mental health services fought and won a battle to forward only codes rather than names to the state. This should reinforce patients' rights. Thus, one can also argue that the law to forward to the state case records of children who receive financial help is against their constitutional rights. It is discriminatory, since children who are supported by their parents do not need to be reported. Again, the receiver of service is discriminated against.

The Law Requiring Keeping Records and Reporting to the State, with Special Emphasis on Children

The Supreme Court majority's ruling in the case of James v. New York State represents the same spirit that prevails in many laws requiring that records for the hospitalized mentally ill be accessible to the state. They reflect fear, prejudice and punitiveness. They are arbitrary, based on no scientific evidence as to which mentally ill persons have to be protected against themselves, as opposed to which mentally ill persons may be dangerous to society. Are the mentally ill who are hospitalized more dangerous to themselves and/or others than those who are not? These laws are often contradictory, and reflect the paternalism that attempts to protect people against themselves.

The laws about children for whom agencies have to keep records or to furnish data to the state represent the same contradiction of protection versus intrusion. They are often neither logical, ethical nor protective; for example, names of undernourished, blind or deaf children in hospitals or institutions do not have to be provided to the state, as contrasted with the names of neglected children. Do we always know that undernourishment, .blindness or deafness is not a result of neglect? What about the right of the infant that enters the world deaf as a result of his mother's lack of prenatal care? Are we sure that once these handicapped children have been placed, their parents will not neglect them? We do know that children, with or without emotional or physical handicaps, are abandoned by their parents whether they are or are not reported to the state. Keeping records in itself does not insure that parents carry out responsibilities to their children. At times record keeping contributes to parents' abandonment of their children in placement, since the records are mainly used to hold them to their financial responsibilities.

The Rights of Children and Their Protection

In social work, the poor carry the burden of research, suffering infringement upon their constitutional rights. That the research is often carried out with the aim to help them only complicates the ethical question of means versus ends. Research about children is even more complicated. Children obviously cannot give consent, yet their rights are at stake. Since research about children is needed, informed consent by a third party is important.[19]

The concept of the "rights of children" is new in the history of mankind. It is even less clearly defined than the "rights of man." Children were until recently considered chattel belonging to their parents. Laws that may exist to protect them are often unclear or unenforced. Children can be pawns in complex adult ploys, as in divorce proceedings or community control of the public schools. One is therefore justified in asking whether parents are always the best qualified to give informed consent. The parents who give consent are often from an economically and socially deprived class. Their life experience, their economic situation, hardly give them the freedom to know, and to weigh, the implications their decision to consent might have in the life of their children. Do they question the effect of constant observation upon the growth process and future development? Do they question what it might do to children if they find themselves written up as cases in a scientific book? In some scientific articles names of the subjects are not even disguised.

Agencies that carry out research to improve their practice are also not the best or only ones qualified to be the third party that gives consent.[20] They have an obvious conflict of interest between service to the child in their care and the interest of other or future children. Also, social work agencies do not have the power to avoid publicizing their recommendations. For example, there are reports by the media regarding the rights of biological versus foster parents in adoption cases. This kind of publicity is a flagrant violation of the child's right as a person, and would not be allowed in a criminal case. Clearly, the adults' wish is given preference.

Accountability and the importance of an involved and alert public in providing for children's emotional and economic security are crucial and deserve encouragement. But whether the children involved are served well by the attendant publicity is questionable.

The Conflicting Needs for Personal Privacy and Personal History

There is the issue of accountability to children, especially those children abandoned by their parents—the "children in limbo." Agencies have to review and carefully decide what kind of records to keep for children while they are responsible for them. I suggest that a system be instituted for children in placement similar to that for children or adults receiving outpatient treatment in mental health clinics; a code could be submitted to the state. The code might include, besides reasons for placement and treatment plan, periodical data for review of the case. This should help to ensure that children do not get lost, and to assess whether the treatment plan has been carried out. Incorporated in the information accompanying the code should be a procedure that will make sure that no file remains with the agency once service is finished.

The public and the professional have to be careful that the concept of accountability is not used to punish people through unconstitutional means. We still have too many laws and regulations in public welfare in general and specifically in the field of child welfare that reflect a punitive attitude toward the poor. We still operate under the influence of the Elizabethan poor law. Is the price for shelter, food, clothing, education—the provision of basic needs—curtailing the right of privacy and protection from the public eye?

It is important to remember that the keeping of records in social work was not begun for malicious reasons or for invasion of privacy. It was done for accountability to the taxpayer, for betterment of service, and for research. Within the social context of the time, the principles of accountability and responsibility and respect for the dignity of the person were courageous. However, in respecting and sharpening these principles for our age, the means no longer fit the end. Life has become more complex. We have greater privacy and freedom and people are more aware of their rights, in contrast to the ancient concept of people belonging to the state. Yet the danger exists that the newly, but not fully, won freedom of a person in his own right will be destroyed by technology before it can be fully experienced.

To combat this, all helping professions and the public have the obligation to guard zealously the person's right to personal privacy and to privacy of those experiences that had or have significance to him. What is being neglected in setting up our elaborate machines is the concept of accountability to the client. The first principle within accountability is answerability. That means protection of our clients' privacy. The continued development of the computer system mandates that we review and revise our record system. Otherwise we will violate the principle of answerability to clients.

What Should the Child's Record Contain?

Some children tell the new worker in the placement agency, "Why tell you? You can read it all in the record." The meaning of records, especially for children, should be explored in depth. To my mind the child's remark has a belligerent tone; it expresses hurt and a sense of dehumanization. It is often used in the service of resistance, originating in desperation, especially by children who have an endless change of workers and placement. For those children, "the pawns in the game of change," the record could also mean a point of identity to which they hold. Somebody wrote about them, so somebody knows. For those who are in limbo the record may be proof that they exist, they are real. Since a record usually has a negative connotation, (e.g., police record), since a record is faceless, not open to the one it is about, one can assume that the record is part of these children's identity, and a negative identity seems better than none. This kind of negative identity fits with the attachment to the institution, the agency, that many of these children feel. It is an impersonal attachment, replacing attachment to persons, which for a variety of reasons they would or could not form. Again, this attachment seems to fulfill a function; it is better than feeling nothing toward a person or an object.

I have argued against keeping records about a child because it is an invasion of his privacy, an infringement upon his constitutional rights.

Yet, as stated previously, for the children in placement who are the wards of an agency, records serve an important purpose; in a sense the records are family history. But the current records do not serve this purpose and do not provide for the possibility of positive identity formation.[21]

Children for whom the agency acts in loco parentis, who have no parents to tell them about their childhood, would like to be like other children and have what other children have. I concur with a students' suggestion that the child's record include, besides vital statistics, the first tooth, the first hair, photographs of the child during his childhood, and school reports.[22] All through his placement the child should be involved and know what is in the record. That in itself is an important educational task. The child is thus treated as a person; he is actively engaged in all possible aspects of treatment. His thoughts and feelings are involved in exploring what is important and meaningful to him and what is not, what should be included in his file and what should be left out.

When the child leaves the agency, his record would be handed to him. Leaving the agency means he has come of age. Even if, as is often the case, the agency continues to pay for his education, he may take his record. The child's vital statistics would be enough to maintain in the agency records.

Such a personal history for one's own keeping might have meaning as positive identity; at least in some aspects the child would be like other children. When he courts a girl, or when she courts a boy, there will be something to show. When their children ask, "What were you like?" they can take out the record and their children will know some of their parents' history.

Notes and References

1. Mary Richmond. What Is Social Casework? Russell Sage Foundation: New York, 1922.

2. Gordon Hamilton. Principles of Social Case Recording. Columbia University Press: New York, 1946.
3. John Frings; Ruth Kratovil and Bernice Polemis. An Assessment of Social Casework Recording: An Experimental Study in Two Family Agencies." Family Service Association of America: New York, 1958.
4. Ibid., p. 76.
5. The view of the caseworker about the purpose of keeping records and their usefulness is similar to the view of physicians expressed in the two papers: Joseph Stokes III, "Is The Patient's Record More Important Than The Patient?", "A Survey: Record Keeping—A Medical Obsession," in Medical Opinion, Vol. 2, 2, February 1973. Keeping of records is important for disciplined thinking of students. In the survey of physicians' attitudes about record keeping, 65% of private physicians and 60% of hospital physicians saw the record as a tool for their own practice and care of the individual patient. Of the hospital physicians, only 14% saw the record as physician-to-physician communication.
6. New York City has state and city laws, as well as administrative rules, requiring the keeping of records. In a cursory poll I found all caseworkers and two out of three administrators ignorant on this issue. All those asked worked in placement agencies.
7. Records are kept by all helping professions except the clergy. The keeping of records is also looked at by professionals and institutions as a means of defense against malpractice suits. I have no reservation about the right of the professional to protect himself. How this can be done without ignoring the ethical question, I do not feel qualified to answer.
8. Child guidance clinics in New York won an important battle with the state. They refused to give names of patients for purpose of reimbursement. One major argument: clients were not told. Yet these same clinics keep clients' records after treatment is terminated. The law requires that child welfare agencies furnish the names of children who enter placement, so that the agencies can be reimbursed. Reports sent to the state about outpatients of hospitals or mental hygiene clinics do not require names of patients. The records can be destroyed after they are audited by the state.
9. A student of mine contacted a prestigious institute in New York City. This institute, engaged in family treatment, uses films and tapes that are shown all over the country to professional audiences for learning purposes. Yet this institute had no material as to how the subjects' agreement to be filmed or appear in a live session before an audience affected their lives.
10. It has been pointed out with validity that some research opinion polls are helpful to their subjects. Side benefits for the subjects are the opportunity to express feelings, concern, and to exert some influence on issues they have convictions about. On the other hand, in treatment, some probably consent to research out of fear that they will otherwise not be treated.
11. See John Fletcher. "Patient Consent for Medical Research," The Hastings Center Studies, Vol. 1, 1, 1973.

12. After writing this paper, I came across Sara Sanborn's article, "An American Family," in Commentary, Vol. 55, 5, May 1973. It is essential reading, as is Donald P. Warwick's "Tea Room Trade: Means and Ends in Social Research," in The Hastings Center Studies, Vol. 1, 1, 1973.

13. Erik Erikson. Insight and Responsibility, W. W. Norton, New York, 1964, p. 5.

14. Lloyd Setleis. Guidelines for the Use of the Tape Recorder as a Tool in Social Work Practice and Education. Mimeographed, Yeshiva University.

15. Morton Teicher, "Let's Abolish the Social Service Exchange." Social Work Journal, Vol. 35, 1, January 1952.

16. Ad in NASW News, April 1973.

17. "Caseworker, Friend or Sleuth," The Social Service Review, Vol. 45, June 1971, pp. 211-213.

18. Ibid.

19. In the medical field, the question of what is involved in patients' consent (adults) is eloquently argued by Fletcher, "Patient's Consent for Medical Research." His findings and recommendations have application to the use of social work research. Since a good deal of research is done about children and underprivileged adolescents, his recommendations about a third party can be used as a basis to think through this issue. Children cannot give consent.

20. Esther Appelberg. "The Significance of Personal Guardianship for Children in Casework," in Sourcebook of Teaching Materials on the Welfare of Children, Council of Social Work Education, New York, 1969. Also in Child Welfare, Vol. XLIX, 1, January 1973. Also in On Fostering, Child Welfare League of America, New York 1972. The issue relevant here: Every child in placement, whose sole guardian is the agency or who is the ward of the state, should have a guardian outside the agency, who could be the child's advocate against the agency, if necessary.

21. Esther Appelberg. "The Dependent Child and the Changing Worker," Child Welfare, July 1969, Vol. XLVIII, 7.

22. Paula Sear, graduate student in my seminar on the Philosophy of Social Work, Wurzweiler School of Social Work, Yeshiva University, New York, spring 1973.

Social Work Education

Introduction

A rereading of the two articles by Esther Appelberg that follow stirred memories of her as my caring and demanding professor (although frequently she seemed more like my demanding and caring professor.) Published in 1965, "Mothers as Social Work Students" deals with crucial issues related to the roles and needs of women. Written ahead of its time, the article remains pertinent and incisive today. Amid the careful scrutiny of detail about the motivation and competence of married women, there suddenly emerges this comment about the younger student: "Young, inexperienced students . . . in applying to schools of social work, usually emphasize a desire to help others. One wonders if this sometimes may be mere lip service to the professed value of the profession, on the assumption that altruism is an entrance ticket to the profession." There is a characteristic sparkle of Dr. Appelberg's wit here, the amalgam of compassion for the young student's desire to gain "entrance" with a sophisticated appreciation that the "desire to help" represents an extension of the evasions and pat answers he has mastered as scars of his education. In that one line, we understand something of her familiarity with power, desperation, and the capacity for corruption in us all.

Her characteristic concerns, of course, inform both articles. Her respect for the women she interviewed, their "having been actively and successfully engaged" with their families, lends depth to our sense of their transition to professional service, and substance to her claims for the meaning of social work education. For example, in "Teaching Casework From Students' Own Material," she states that "the aim of professional education is the development of independent thinking, flexibility of mind, curiosity and inquiry." The emphatic word here is "development," and it strikes me as the crucial dimension of her gift for teaching, the ability to allow the student to create his own learning system. As she had noted, "a major aspect of casework is the meaning and timing of reassurance," and, as learners, the "use of one's own case can be anxiety-producing." The capacity she had, and about which her students felt grateful, was ability to let us experience our differences, with the concomitant pain and confusion, while giving us the unspoken sense that what we learned would help us "stand up for our work and our convictions."

Alan Bernstein

Teaching Casework from Students' Own Material

To the best of my knowledge, casework is taught from teaching records in most schools of social work on this continent. Students' own cases are used as a teaching medium mostly in the field in supervision. Yet the students' own case record, where utilized, provides an important tool for teaching casework in the classroom, in the practice course.

It also has applicability for inservice training in the agencies, since it differs from group supervision or case conference, which often focuses on problem solving. This paper concerns the rationale for teaching casework from students' own cases, and describes how the rationale was developed. It deals also with course content for the first year's sequence of casework, the conceptualization of the process, and the use of teaching and other media.

Rationale [1]

Social casework demands that the student give help before he understands the nature of professional help. He does not yet have adequate knowledge about human behavior and its psychological influ-

---

Published originally in CHILD WELFARE, L, 10, December 1971.

ences in the taking and giving of help. He is called upon to be a helper at the same time that he himself needs help. Only gradually does he understand what he is doing. Like his client, he experiences helplessness. He finds himself in a position where conflicting demands, such as dependency-independency needs, touch his personality, which then has to undergo a change so that the conflict can be resolved constructively. Where the objective is to teach students how to be caseworkers, the case method of student presentations offers the students, as well as the teacher, an opportunity to learn and to teach from the immediacy of the students' own material that reflects their current learning, understanding and ability. The material also gives the other students a chance to identify aspects of their own learning and questioning with those of their colleagues.

My first experience in teaching casework from students' own case records was in Israel. We had just introduced the teaching of casework to the Israeli schools and found that unless we used teaching material from the United States, we would have to use the students' own material. The students were the only ones asked to use process, in contrast to workers, most of whom were in public assistance, recording actions only in behalf of clients. At the Wurzweiler School of Social Work, Yeshiva University, I found that the students' recordings were the main tool used in the practice classes. "Class and field instruction are integrated and provide continuity in learning and progression from the simple to the more complex. . . . In this practice the student learns to utilize professional methods and to apply his increasing knowledge in the most effective manner." [2]

Theory and Content: Its Use in the Classroom

Teaching first-year casework means teaching students from the negative, since their records do not present exemplary practice. On the other hand, one has the advantage of starting where the students are in the field, that is, at the first-year students' own beginning. This provides a common bond among students: All are about equal, and they are not swamped by insight. They can identify with the opportunity to see change and growth through their classmates' material, which in turn reinforces their own image. It is hard to grasp and put into practice the concepts behind such questions as: How do you start with a client whom you see for the first time? What do we mean by a professional relationship, as opposed to a personal one? If you have parents with children, whom do you see first?

Classes are arranged so that they have a fairly good representation of the different field placements. This enables the students to obtain understanding of a variety of settings. Usually the first two sessions focus on students' expectations from the course, how they feel about going into the field and meeting the clients, the instructor's expectations of them, and how the class will be conducted.

The first assignment relates to their first meeting with their client:

> Present on half a page who your first client was and what was his request. Write a brief paper on the thoughts and feelings that come to you in this helping process. The completed paper—interview and your own material—should not be more than four pages, including any questions you have. This is due immediately after you have had the first interview.

Usually the students will not yet have been in the field when this assignment is discussed with them. In the second class some of the papers are read and discussed. One question that comes up regularly is whether one should read what has been recorded by previous workers. Students are usually split on this issue. Some fear they will be prejudiced, others hope it will help them to get facts and to be better prepared for the interview. Underlying these questions is the student's uncertainty about his being a student and becoming a worker. In other words, what will he do with the facts and feelings and how will he use himself? The new situation can be uncomfortable. The method also helps to focus on a theme that will be present throughout the year—the relationship between facts and feelings, or in Erikson's words, the "nature of the evidence." There are facts that can be established, and facts that are more in the nature of client's subjective feelings. In the first category are sex, age, occupation. The second category might include the case of a woman who says that her daughter shouts at her, but in fact she may or may not be shouting; the tone makes the music. The daughter might deny the shouting, since she whispers. This whisper might be more devastating than any shouting. What can be learned is that something negative is going on between mother and daughter. Such a situation highlights for the student how he feels about this relationship to which he is exposed.

Usually some students have not yet seen their first client. For them, the first assignment is changed. Since their papers might be overly influenced by class discussion, the original assignment would no longer be a learning experience. These students are asked to write their thoughts and feelings about not seeing their first clients. Their papers are read and discussed in class. Almost without exception, these reveal that the longer the time lapse before seeing a client, the more the students' anxiety mounts. Often their fears lead to overpreparation.

Both assignments sometimes tend to heighten student fears about the first interview. They worry not only about how they will make out with their clients, but how they will handle their assignment. In other words, they learn early about countertransference, the feeling they bring to the situation, and the restraint they have to put upon themselves to use these feelings in appropriate response to the needs of the client.

Through this way of teaching, it is almost inevitable that students learn early one of the basic principles in casework—the futility of giving quick reassurance. In the discussion at an early stage of feelings about placements, expectations, hopes and disappointments, one student expressed anxiety about his placement, in a hospital for the chronically ill. Another student, who had worked there during the summer, started to reassure him, telling him that after the initial shock it was not so bad as she had expected. Another told him about her own beginning in a setting for mentally retarded, which also turned out not to be so bad as anticipated. But it was obvious that the first student still was anxious about his placement. At that point one of the reassuring students said, "I realize that all our talk and advice does not really help you; you are just as anxious as you were before."

At this point I summed up by pointing out that a major aspect of casework is the meaning and timing of reassurance. The discussion illustrated to the students that feelings can interfere with intellect, that emotions have their own logic, and that the intellect does not always gain the upper hand. "Reassurance" is a concept important to students when they try to reason with their clients.

Using the Teaching Record

Since one goal is to move as quickly as possible into the theory of practice and an understanding of the casework process and its beginning phase, record material is introduced into the class in the third session. It is at this point that use is made of the teaching record, (a) to relieve the tension and anxiety of having to produce simultaneously for field and class; (b) to ease the pressure involved in having to present one's own function at a point when one does not yet know what it is all about. It moves the focus to the content, helping to clarify the role of the social worker, the purpose of casework, and the process. It allows the student to make associations and connections with his own work in a more neutral atmosphere.

This teaching record is a fairly simple one, insofar as we control the complexity of human behavior, the nature of the client and the problem—which of course in practice is not so. The simple case often turns out to be complex, at times recognized as such only by the supervisor, at other times, also by the student. The simple case serves as a model of what the caseworker does, the people he helps, and the function of his agency. It helps the student relate back to the earlier discussions of principles and issues.

Introducing Students' Recording

Usually at the end of the fourth class, after at least some of the students have seen their clients, a volunteer is asked to bring in the first interview. Whatever the case or setting, the first student case and subsequent early ones provide an opportunity to return to the student's beginning effort as a functioning caseworker.

Cases are brought from various settings so that the class can experience the variety of people who come to agencies—ages, stages of personality development, problems and situations—and the variety of disciplines with which social workers work—teachers, physicians, psychologists, nurses, childcare workers, homemakers. The student cases highlight the way the philosophy of an agency influences work with a client, and how the caseworker functions in accordance with professional ethics, principles, and knowledge. Through conceptualization and formulation of casework principles, students learn to understand the uniqueness of every client, and the dynamics and approaches involved. Since they are using their own cases and since the first assignment has sensitized them, they early become aware of the meaning of the professional relationship and the nature of transference and countertransference.

It is specified that during the year there will be cases that illustrate work with a victim of the Nazi holocaust, and with minority groups such as the blacks and Puerto Ricans. The case of the victim of the Nazis gives students the opportunity to observe what is specifically Jewish in the experience of persecution and immigration, and to determine the social worker's role in helping these victims, with emphasis on what this experience means to the victim's children. The problems of immigration and migration, with examples of Cubans, Puerto Ricans, and the Southern blacks coming to New York, are taken up. The experiences of persecution, uprooting and formation of identity are discussed from the perspective of the social worker.

The cases of the Jew, the black, and the Puerto Rican enable the student to look at clients whose social class may differ from his own; at economics, use of social welfare programs, and dissimilarity of race, ethnic culture and religion, as these might affect relationships between worker and client. It enables the class to weave current problems of social casework into the class material. At times we have had to discuss work with interpreters, since some of the students carried such cases.

All case material facilitates interweaving important casework concepts, even though they might not always come in a 1-2-3 sequence. Contrary to those who advocate sequential learning in casework, it is important to remember the aim of professional education is the development of independent thinking, flexibility of mind, curiosity and inquiry. This of course is different from training that is content- and task-oriented. A teacher must know the content and help students to acquire it, but also must pay attention to them as learners, and to how they begin to master content. In every class parts of their recording are used to develop diagnostic thinking, to illustrate specific psychological points and concepts, and to help them put theory into practice.

After the spring vacation, the cases the students present will include ending with clients, and preparation of their clients for new workers.

The progression does not necessarily move from the simple to the complex case, but relates more to the growing development of the student. Some complain about lack of structure. They experience the process as unstructured because they are forced to find their own structure as learners and future professionals, and not every student is ready for this. It is a high demand, and a difficult experience. The course is, in fact, structured. There are implicit expectations of the students:

1) to assume responsibility for their work;
2) to formulate and present questions clearly;
3) to learn how to share their work;
4) to develop greater trust in themselves and thereby learn to risk what they think, feel, and intend to do in response to the needs of clients;
5) to learn acceptance and use of criticism;
6) to differentiate between learning needs and learning problems.

As the students see themselves within the group exposed to learning, some absorbing it, others not, they experience what it means to clients to take in difference. The opportunity to present their own work parallels their activity with their clients, and they comprehend the meaning of taking and giving help.

The instructor, of course, has to be aware of currents, hostility, over-protectiveness, etc., in the class. At the same time, the approach gives the instructor the opportunity to help the timid student assert himself. Also the student who likes to control or is excessively vocal learns to give others a chance. The students become better listeners, learn to differentiate between debate and discussion, and become aware of their own feelings. They also learn that they differ in their feelings about what they read, hear and experience, and this makes them more open to what the client feels and more aware that he might feel differently from what they thought he ought to feel.

Undoubtedly, the use of one's own case can be anxiety-producing, but anxiety can also occur if the student takes over a case from his supervisor or reads records that describe the work of experienced and gifted workers. The own-case technique is helpful because the student learns to stand up for his work and his convictions. The student learns to accept criticism and be open to suggestions from other students. It helps the student to be more open in expressing his questions, and his agreement and criticism of fellow students' work. It also helps the student to accept supervision. To lower the students' defensiveness, the difference between learning need and learning problem is spelled out early. The learning need is to be expected from all: how to focus, to explore, to understand the meaning behind a client's request, how to end an interview. Learning becomes a problem when students cannot move; for example, the student who prolongs the interview with every client, or who cannot bring himself to find out certain facts about the client. But students understand that they are not graded on their field casework in the classroom—that their records are only a tool.

Conflict in Approaches

A question that comes up without fail about teaching from students' own material is: What if the supervisor has a different approach from the classroom teacher regarding case interpretation or treatment process? Does this not create confusion or conflict and how is it dealt with?

When this situation arose, some supervisors who became alarmed or anxious contacted the school. In such event, differences have to be brought out into the open. It is similar to what a student and supervisor might experience in taking over a case from another worker. The student might be asked to approach the case in a different way. This also can happen in a case consultation or psychiatric consultation at the agency; a parallel situation arises when the student reads literature presenting different points of view.[3] The student has to learn to live with differences of opinion, with ambiguities. If he cannot accept them, how is he going to help his clients to live with ambiguities, to make choices? The responsibility for working with the client rests with the student, and ultimately with the supervisor. The instructor teaches, but does not supervise cases. The student knows he is not held responsible if his interpretation or approach does not coincide with the instructor's, but he is responsible for presenting an intelligent point of view.

At the same time, use of the students' material lends itself to close collaboration between school and agency. If the student's participation in class shows that he is having a learning problem, the instructor can take the matter to the student's faculty adviser, who then can take it up with the field instructor, so that the student gets constructive help.

Teaching from students' material does not preclude use of teaching records, tapes or other media. I use teaching records for some classes to discuss persons or problems not assigned to any student. Observation of conjoint or family interview and discussion afterward has been used to highlight underlying concepts and techniques, since few first-year students are exposed to this. But such media have been used sparingly. The ultimate resource in teaching is the teacher himself, just as the ultimate resource in casework is the conscious use of the worker himself in his relation to the client.

References

1. Virginia P. Robinson, Supervision in Social Casework (Chapel Hill, N.C.: University of North Carolina Press, 1936); Charlotte Towle, "Learner in Education for the Professions," in Education for Social Work (Chicago: University of Chicago Press, 1954); Lloyd Setleis, "Teaching Social Casework Practice: A Social Process," (unpublished dissertation, Philadelphia, 1959); Yonata Feldman, "Learning Through Recorded Material," in H. J. Parad, ed., Ego Psychology and Dynamic Casework (Family Service Association of America, 1958) 203-215; Bertha Reynolds, Learning and Teaching in the Practice of Social Work (New York: Rinehart & Co., 1942).
2. From 1969-71 catalog of the Wurzweiler School of Social Work, Yeshiva University.
3. In one agency where the writer serves as faculty adviser, it was arranged that students share cases with workers, so that they were not exposed only to the view of their supervisor.

Mothers as Social Work Students

The Wurzweiler School of Social Work of Yeshiva University decided to take a fresh approach to the question of mother-as-student. Since its establishment in 1957, the school has seen as one of its important tasks the preparation of married women with children for social work. Based on the knowledge that although many of these women were interested in social work, they were not usually admitted to the schools of social work in the New York area, it was felt that such a program would meet a definite need.

The school felt that these women would be a good source for recruitment, for among other attributes, they had maturity and life experience, and a capacity to understand and to empathize with the difficulties Americans face in setting up a family and rearing children in a complicated world. Furthermore, since most of these women had already established families, they had before them many years of practice in the field that would not be interrupted by marriage and childbirth. Given the value such a program would have for the field, it was clear that some modification would have to be made in its educational time requirements to make it possible for these women to fulfill their home obligations without damage to themselves and

From: Social Work Education Reporter, XIII, 4, December 1965 (New York: Council on Social Work Education) reprinted with permission.

their families. No compromise could be made in the quality of the program. Such a compromise would have meant shortchanging them and shortchanging the field.

The changes in time requirements resulted in the "extended program." Candidates were encouraged to extend their period of study up to a maximum of 5 years. This allowed them to begin by taking academic courses only for a year or 2, thus completing some of the academic course requirements while gradually readjusting to the status of student. When they were ready to enter a full time program, they would have 3 days of field work and practice courses and 1 day of classwork, allowing them to attend school for 4 days a week instead of 5. All degree requirements may be completed in 3, 4 or 5 years.

To appraise this program, it was decided to query these students and determine whether they were satisfied with it; what problems arose; was concern as to the possible negative impact of the mothers' study on their obligations toward their children justified; and would they fulfill the requirements?

Methodology and Results

In this study, a total of 33 married women with children were included.[1] Of these, 13 had received the master of social work degree; 16 were still at various stages of their educational program at the time of the study; and four had dropped out of school. Twenty-nine women were interviewed, four having failed to reply to a letter from the dean asking them to participate. Of the four who failed to respond, one had received her degree, while the other three had withdrawn from the program within 2 to 12 weeks after they had started.[2]

The study was conducted during October and November 1964. Twenty-nine women were interviewed extensively in accordance with a questionnaire that consisted of both objective and open-end questions. All participants were asked to avoid discussing the questions with each other to preclude contamination of responses; confidentiality was assured so that the current students, especially, would not feel concerned that the information would be used in any way for evaluation by the faculty. The interviews lasted from 1 to 1½ hours.

A Profile of the Married Student

Our subjects came from both professional and nonprofessional backgrounds.[3] At the point of their enrollment at Wurzweiler School of Social Work, their average age was 40 years. The duration of their marriages ranged from 3 to 30 years; the average was 14.8 years. The average number of children was two. The age range of the children was 1 year to 26 years, but most were adolescents or young adults.

Of the 29 subjects, eight personally financed their studies and 21 financed their studies through their own resources, plus various scholarships and grants. Many of these were helped through more than one source.[4]

The subjects were asked when they first became interested in social work. Four had become interested while in high school and 13 while in college. That the group of 13 who became interested while in college includes a number of women who attended college after they were already married and had children reaffirms the well established observation that interest in social work tends to develop rather late in life.

Of the 29 subjects, nine had no career ambitions before marriage; 12 reported that they had ambitions; eight of these 12 had been interested in public health, social work, teaching and nursing. Seven had wished to study social work and two of the seven had actually started. Ten had not worked at all before marriage, while 19 had worked. Of those who worked, five worked in social work and six as teachers or nurses. Only one of the 19 students had some idea of going into the field prior to marriage and only two went so far as to start school. These findings indicate that the decision to go into social work is made late in life. Furthermore, only five of the 19 who worked prior to marriage had been in social work.

This picture in general, and employment in social work specifically, changed during their marriages. Twenty-eight of the 29 subjects worked during their marriages, compared with 10 prior to marriage. On the other hand, nine worked in social work during marriage, compared with five before marriage.

The number of subjects engaged in volunteer work was high.

Twenty-two worked in various civic and religious organizations or in parent-teacher associations as fund-raisers, officers, and presidents, while only seven did no volunteer work at all. Nine were actively engaged in direct contact with clients, working in mental hospitals, old age homes, Girl Scout troops, and groupwork agencies.

Motivations and Expectations

What motivated these women and what were their expectations at the point of enrollment; what did they miss in their lives and what were they looking for? To obtain answers, it was felt that open-end questions were most suitable. In analyzing the answers, it was remembered that the subjects were being asked to recall feelings and thoughts that, for some of them, occurred years ago. In this kind of recall, the danger of getting a mixture of poetry and truth is great. Yet as subjects' answers were recorded and analyzed, there seemed to be more truth than poetry in them.

Responses to "Why did you seek professional education at this time?" seemed to fall naturally, though roughly, into three major categories.

Five stated that the wish to become a social worker or other professional had always been at the back of their minds. They felt that now that their children were older and needed them less and their husbands could afford their tuition, it was time to go ahead with realizing their dreams.

Seven responded that they were motivated by a need for financial security, in addition to such other motivations as psychological fulfillment. Staying at home led to frustration and dissatisfaction. They reported: "My first need was for financial security." "I needed to provide myself with something meaningful." "Out of my experience in the Department of Welfare, I had a feeling of inadequacy."

Seventeen subjects (more than half the women interviewed) clearly expressed dissatisfaction and feelings of not being fulfilled psychologically as their only motivation for seeking professional education at this time of their lives. They wanted something for themselves. They felt bored. They saw their husbands busy, their children growing up and needing them less and less. These women expressed themselves very clearly: "I was becoming depressed at this time; it was not enough to shop and to go to matinees." "Life was passing me by." "I observed my mother and other women." "I had gone for some help myself and it was suggested that I start to look into what I wanted."

One theme seems to run through all three categories: dissatisfaction, insecurity, feeling of not being needed, feeling of being useless, of being passed by, left out, ignored. Variations on this theme all suggest the self-concern of this group in seeking professional education.

These women expressed, to some degree, what Betty Friedan described in *The Feminine Mystique*.[5] However, they did not find housework demeaning drudgery. They were not uninterested in bringing up their children themselves; they enjoyed child rearing, but having been actively and successfully engaged in these areas, they found themselves with plenty of time on their hands now that the children were growing up and attending school, and household activities routinized and mechanized. Sitting at home and waiting for the children and husband to return from school and work was not enough. Once the children no longer needed constant care, these women felt that there was still much they could give and wanted to give; they wanted to find takers for what they had to offer. Their volunteer activities were often routinized and not stimulating. Often, working with professionals, they felt they could perform better and find more satisfaction if they themselves became professionals.

Feeling less needed and observing other women (their mothers), they were afraid of becoming like them, of becoming dissatisfied and a burden on their surroundings. They were trying to adjust to changing conditions. Their readiness to do so in spite of many conventional obstacles, hardships, and fears, is an indication of strength and maturity.

Psychotherapy seemed to be an important factor in the decision to go into social work. Half the respondents indicated that they had been in therapy before enrolling at the school and 11 subjects asserted that therapy had influenced their decision to take up social work and to apply at this time.

Fourteen were continuing in various kinds of psychotherapy at the time of the study. Fifty percent is a high percentage to have been in therapy. It is a far higher rate than for the general population and probably far greater than for other helping professions such as teaching, psychology, or even psychiatry. It is a safe guess that half the psychoanalysts have not undergone psychoanalysis *before* beginning their own training.

Whatever their reasons for undergoing treatment, they were also motivated by a feeling that they were not using themselves to the full extent of their capacities and wanted to do so. That 11 of the 14 chose to go into social work while undergoing therapy clearly indicates this trend.[6]

In looking for a solution to their problems our subjects evidenced a high level of sophistication and a high level of self-awareness and motivation regarding the availability and use of professional help. Since the absence of illness is not an absolute criterion of health, and since one of the basic assumptions in social work is that the ability to use and take help is a sign of strength, members of the profession can only be impressed.

In order to learn more about the reasons for the subjects' choice of social work and their knowledge of the nature of social work at the time of choice, we asked: "What did you think social work was?" and "What were your expectations?"

In response to "What did you think social work was?", 10 revealed that their knowledge at the time of choice was rather vague. Responses included: "helping people" and "a form of bringing about justice." Nineteen (two-thirds) revealed a more sophisticated knowledge, answering: "helping children in whatever difficulties they have in social or family relations" and ". . . I realized these were more than money problems."

Responses to "What were your expectations?" could be divided roughly into three categories:

Three of the respondents were "present oriented." "Mostly my thoughts were centered on my own feelings—how will I react—will I be able to take it?" "It was going to be more fun than staying at home."

Seven subjects saw the present tied in with the future. They stressed personal fulfillment, the development of their own personalities as differentiated from taking care of their families. "I expected certain satisfactions from this field during the years my children would not be around." "It makes me feel more of a person."

The majority, two-thirds, held expectations in terms of gaining knowledge, acquiring a degree, increased income, or emotional security. "I think it will give me a degree." ". . . to have an intellectual leg to stand on."

Although the responses were varied and had different levels of sophistication, all replies indicated a common denominator, the fulfillment of personal needs.

Since the Wurzweiler School is interested in preparing its students to work in Jewish agencies, it was helpful to know if the factor of Jewishness influenced the students' choice.[7] In answer to the question, "Why did you choose a Jewish school?" Jewishness seemed an important factor for half of our subjects. The other half were attracted primarily by "smallness of school," "the possibility of the extended program," "low tuition," or "no reasons at all."

What Happens to the Students at School During Their Study?

A reason frequently given for denying admission to schools of social work is the subjects' age; older students are considered a poor risk. To see whether or not this assumption was justified, we compared dropout rates, length of attendance, school grades, and anxieties for women without children enrolled in the regular program and women with children enrolled in the special, extended program. The length of time students with children took to complete degree requirements ranged from 2 to 5 years; the average time was 3 years. Dropouts showed no significant statistical difference between women without children and those with children; women with children did not withdraw any more frequently than women without children.[8]

Undergraduate and graduate school grades were compared within each group and between both groups. The average undergraduate grade for *both* groups was almost exactly midway between B and C, and the average graduate grade was almost exactly B.[9] There was no significant difference in achievement between the two groups.

Thus it seems that concern about other students being a poor risk is not valid. The older, married student group proved to be no greater risk than other female students.

What kinds of anxieties did this group of women with children have while attending school? They were asked, "What were some of the most dominant anxieties you had while attending school?" Perhaps surprisingly, anxiety because of concern for their families was expressed by only six subjects. They expressed guilt as mothers. "They would look at school as negative—as having taken their mothers away." "My child fell. Would this have happened if I had been there?" "I wonder how my sick child feels if I do not take him, but take another child, to the doctor?" Fourteen others, however, reported anxiety only in regard to their role as students. "I had higher expectations of myself than I would have had as a younger or less experienced person." "The anxiety was around my own performance." Nine respondents did not report any anxiety at all.

It surprised these investigators that only a minority of our subjects questioned their dual role as parents and students. The hypothesis that the majority would be troubled by their dual role as mother and student did not hold true probably because most of the students were just beginning the program or attending on a part-time basis, so that the consequences for themselves and their families were not yet deeply felt. This might also explain why respondents did not report any anxieties.

What Happens to Their Families?

It is obvious that when a mother returns to school, her decision will affect her family. If this decision is a mutual one and the family views it favorably, adverse repercussions during the mother's course of study may be kept to a minimum.

In answer to the question, "Did you confer with your husband and children before you decided to return to school, and what were their reactions to your plan?", all subjects reported that they had conferred with their husbands. Only four husbands were "neutral" or "not interested." Most husbands were encouraging, pledging financial and all other kinds of help and support.

Eight subjects did not discuss their plans with their children, either because the children were too young or because they did not consider it appropriate. Of the 21 who discussed their plans with their children, only a few found that their children raised objections or were afraid that they would "lose out;" the great majority of the children were enthusiastic. This latter group, however, was not always clear about the implications of their mothers' plans.

How helpful was this family discussion and how did the pledges of help stand up? How did our subjects' study affect their children? In answer to the question, "Were there any changes in your relations with your husband as a consequence of your returning to school?", one reported a change for the worse; three reported that the change resulted in a crisis that led them to better readjustment; 14 reported no change; 11 reported a change without a crisis, leading to a deepening of the relationship, with greater give and take. Husband and wife came closer together. Husbands had greater appreciation of their wives as persons. They read books on the wives' reading lists and "widened their horizons."

In answer to the question, "Were there any changes in your children, as a consequence of your returning to school?", three reported a change for the worse, 10 reported no change, and 16 reported a change for the better.[10] The mothers' enrollment in graduate school seemed to highlight problems and typical areas of concern natural to the children's age. On the other hand, some mothers seemed to be able to deal with some of these same concerns in a better way. They reported: "Less involvement with children." "Makes children less dependent." They also reported that knowledge gained in school helped them with their children. Children took pride in their mothers, reflected in the children's improved educational goals.

In answer to the item, "Was the relation between your husband and children affected while you attended school?", two reported a change for the worse. "He tried so hard to protect me, to make it possible to study, that he clashed with the children." Eleven reported no change, while 13 reported a change for the better. "He has become closer to them." "He developed more understanding about the children." Contrary to the women's own fears and the customary demur by schools that mothers' attendance might be detrimental to their family life, the effect in the great majority of cases was change for the better in their relationships with their husbands and with their children, as well as between husband and children.

This change for the better held true despite diminution in the usual social life of subjects and their families. One would have surmised that cutting down on social activities might bring disharmony, but it was not so. In answer to the item, "How was your social life affected by attending school?", 24 reported that it was "affected dramatically," but a typical comment was: "We were excited with what we were doing; husbands did not resent it."

Such responses to queries about the effects of study on family life indicated that these were women who had achieved a sense of their own identity, whose family life was good, and who were able to discuss important decisions with their husbands and children. This mutuality in their family lives was, without question, a factor in their success as students. It was surprising that subjects did not always report awareness of any change. Some professed not to have thought about it, but then went on to report and describe changes.

After Graduation

All 12 graduates interviewed answered "yes" to the question, "Have you fulfilled your expectations since leaving school?" They felt that: "I got the knowledge I wanted"; "I have gone beyond my expectations." All of them are currently employed in social work.[11]

Seven felt that their education changed their attitude toward Judaism in a positive direction. They mentioned their ability to use what they learned with clients, more academic understanding, more identification as a Jew and feeling more comfortable being with some Jews. Five reported no change. Since "Jewishness" was a factor in applying to the Wurzweiler School for only four of the 12 who were graduated, it is obvious that for this group attendance at Wurzweiler School of Social Work made a positive change in their attitude toward Judaism.

What did 2 years of graduate education give these women besides the satisfaction of having accomplished their professional goal, of becoming active in their chosen profession? Did their educational experience fulfill their "personal expectations" of development as persons in their own right, of fulfillment? Furthermore, does social work education make for a change in the attitudes of its students? In hope of gaining insight into this area, we asked: "Do you feel that you are a different person as a consequence of being a social worker?" To this question, all 12 subjects responded affirmatively, and pointed out changes in themselves and in their families. "I used to be very defensive and insecure; I have learned to be myself." "I have direction, so has my family." "It made me more human, but the consequences are so great, when you feel that way, you are really human." ". . . the blinders are off, it would be pretty hard not to make changes."

Summary and Conclusion

A group of married women with children, graduated from or currently enrolled in the "extended program" of the Wurzweiler School of Social Work, was studied to determine their success as students. Their average age was 40 and the average number of children was two. The graduates completed their degree requirements in 3 years on the average. Their grades showed some improvement over the grades they had achieved at college and their dropout rate was no higher than that of the rest of the female student population, with some indication that the dropout rate of married women may be lower. All graduates have been working since graduation.

The majority had discussed their plans of school attendance with their families and received their full cooperation while attending school. On the whole, school attendance seemed to have had a positive effect on their family life.

The group was highly sophisticated and well motivated, with a deep sense of self-awareness. Outstanding was the clearly voiced expectation that social work as a profession would fulfill their own needs. Their strength and maturity were evidenced in the open expression of these desires. This awareness that in choosing a profession one is entitled to fulfill one's own needs and to obtain gratification differentiates these subjects from young, inexperienced students. The latter, in applying to schools of social work, usually emphasize a desire to help others. One wonders if this sometimes may be mere lip service to the professed value of the profession, on the assumption that altruism is an entrance ticket to the profession. This recalls Murray and Kluckhohn's reference to ". . . the tendency for society to press the individual to the utmost for renunciation of 'self-interest' and acceptance of 'sacrifice and service.' By definition, a highly socialized person is just like the majority, the average. Constructive social innovations and intellectual and artistic creations will hardly come from such individuals." [12]

One is inclined to predict that married women with children, regardless of age, who are clear about their motivation, who have thought through and discussed their plans with their families, are good risks for social work education. They are a valuable resource for the field of social work.

References

1. The group included group workers and caseworkers, divorcees and widows.
2. In presenting the data, it will be noted that the number of subjects vary. This is a result of the non-applicability to the entire group of some of the questions.
3. Social class of the subjects was established according to the occupation of the husband. Eighteen women belonged to Class I (Doctors, Lawyers, Rabbis, Engineers, Social Workers, etc.), 15 to Class II (Clerks, Self-Employed Businessmen, Public Welfare Workers, etc.).
4. The sources were: New York State Scholarship Incentive Award, Yeshiva University Tuition Scholarships, Federation of Jewish Philanthropies Scholarships, National Institute of Mental Health, New York State Department of Mental Health, National Association of Jewish Center Workers, and Agency Commitments.
5. Betty Friedan. The Feminine Mystique (New York: Bell Publishing Co., Inc., 1963).
6. This finding is the same as reported by Margaret J. Rioch, et al., NIMH Pilot Study in Training Mental Health Counselors, American Journal of Orthopsychiatry, 33, 4 (July 1963), pp. 678, 679. In another program for married women with children for mental health counselors, 100% of the trainees had previously undergone psychotherapy. (Oral communication.)
7. Three subjects were not Jewish.
8. However, there was a trend (10 percent level) for the group with children to have fewer dropouts.
9. The differences between undergraduate and graduate grades were not statistically computed because of differences in grading systems in various undergraduate schools and the graduate school.
10. The question did not apply to 3 subjects.
11. Two reported that they were looking for better jobs.
12. Clyde Kluckhohn and Henry A. Murray, eds., with David M. Schneider, Personality in Nature, Society, and Culture, Second Edition, Revised and Enlarged. (New York: Alfred A. Knopf, 1959), p. 48.

Holocaust and Immigration

Introduction

Modern industrial society is characterized by mobility of peoples, rootlessness, and man's cruelty to man. The Nazi holocaust was unparalleled in the intensity of its brutality and in its impeccable attention to detail. However scarred, the survivors represent a unique experience. Their very survival constitutes an existential reality that must be confronted by those who did not share that experience. Esther Appelberg has probed this area with clarity and inner pain. In her work in the displaced persons camps, smuggling children to the nascent state of Israel through the British blockade, and later with children in Israel who knew no families, she felt and experienced their struggles and their sadness. Dr. Appelberg could conceptualize the problem on the highest intellectual level, and simultaneously work in the most intimate and feeling manner with the client who had the problem. Some of her best work was with the most deprived children, who suffered complete separation from mothering persons. Both the youngsters of Youth Aliyah and the American children at Bellefaire needed nurturance on an anaclitic level. Rarely do we find this capacity for sensitive nurturing treatment and rigorous intellectual objectivity in the same person.

The letter to D. . . . that begins this section is an example of her work; the case (Mrs. D.) is later referred to in the article "Holocaust Survivors and Their Children." Incidentally, Dr. Appelberg never did

133

close this case. She continued contact with this young woman, even arranging for a friend to "give her away" at her wedding, so that she would know she was cherished and had meaning to someone.

The article on her experience as a foreign student has relevance to all those who work with the rootless, the mobile populations, immigrants, and refugees in a world that has become filled with transients. In the process of geographical movement, they often lose contact with their cultural and emotional roots and those who work with them tend to deny their heritage. Like many of Dr. Appelberg's statements, it is specific and yet universal. We can all learn and teach from these experiences.

Naomi Abramowitz
Ramat Gan, Israel

(Editor's note: The following letters are part of a correspondence between Dr. Appelberg and a young woman who was a holocaust survivor cared for by Youth Aliyah.)

1965

Dear Esther—Many greetings:

I got your letter and to tell the truth I wasn't pleased with it at all. Moreover I got a shock when I read its content. Esther, when I wrote to you that I am looking for my relatives, I didn't think for a moment that you had already tried to do that for me. I think you should have told me so—that you looked for relatives for me—because then I would have come to terms, if this is possible, to come to terms, that I remained without parents or relatives and who knows if my name is really my name or that Youth Aliya gave me this name—that I won't be a girl without a name.

Esther, I'm sorry, but my letter is very confused because I don't know how to write to you or what I want to tell you. You don't know how much I would like to have you near me so that you could help me to get over my mood—my very bad mood—which has hit bottom—and I'm all confused completely.

Esther, I always wanted to get close to you—more than I succeeded —and I don't know if you felt this feeling I had for you. Don't be surprised if I write to you that I tried to find in you a substitute for my dead mother. I don't know how you will receive what you will read in this letter, but insofar as I insulted you, I am asking for your forgiveness—and you should know that not out of bad intention did I do that, but I simply wanted you to know how I feel.

Esther, I am very sorry I started to look for my relatives without knowing that you know already, more or less, the results of my efforts in this search. It is possible that if I would have known what you know I would not have tried to search for relatives.

Esther, I think that I'll end for today. We all feel fine. A is also fine even though she lost a lot of weight. Let's hope that everything will be OK.

Yours, waiting for an answer.

D

Regards from my family.

1965

Dear D,

Thanks for your letter. I was pleased to hear from you and am sorry that your daughter was so sick. I can imagine how much you worried about her. The pain of bringing up children. It is good that she recovered, did she gain weight?

I understand very well that you want to know more about your parents, and relatives, and that you want to see whether they are still alive. When I first met you, I tried to find your parents and relatives. I understood how important this was to you, even though you could not talk about it, as it was too painful. I never told you this, you were not ready, the wound was too big. After I went to the department of missing relatives—I did not tell you that I did it—I could not find out anything, so there was nothing I could tell you. I am afraid that now you too will not find any clues. It is almost a quarter of a century since you were taken by force from your parents.

What can I say to comfort you? That now you have a good and beautiful family of your own? That you have a delightful daughter? That in my opinion you tell her, if she should ask you, that there was a terrible disaster, that you were taken by force from your parents, but that you come from good parents, "parents that loved me;" because how else could you now be such a devoted mother.

With pleasure I shall send you a picture of me, I'll have one taken this week. But I did not want to hold up this letter. I wanted you to know meanwhile that the relation between us is important to me—the relation to you, your daughter and your husband.

I'll finish for today. If you have time and feel like it, write again.

Warm greetings to you and your family. With blessing.

Yours,

Esther

The Foreign Student and the American Casework Supervisor

This is in part a protest, and in part a sorting out of what had meaning for me in the initial stage as a foreign student and what was helpful to me. It is written after I have finished my first year of training in a school for social work and is my personal experience. It is a reflection of a positive experience, and it is the result of discussion with supervisor and advisor, with foreign and American students.

I finished Teachers College 8 years ago. In the course of this training, I held a part-time job teaching neglected and underprivileged children. After graduation, I was assigned to set up a new school in a new small settlement in the Upper Galilee, where living conditions were primitive. I remained there for almost a year. Upon my return to Jerusalem, I worked in a youth trade union, having the responsibility to safeguard rights such as employment, sick leave, vacations and wages for working adolescents between the ages of 14 and 18. I also helped them to plan for their further educational and vocational training in evening classes. I participated in setting up a school for girls who wanted to become dressmakers, and sat in on a supervisory committee. I taught there once a week. After 2 years, I was sent to Germany by the Jewish Agency for Palestine, where we were a

* Written when the author was a master's degree candidate in November 1952.

subunit to United Nations Relief and Rehabilitation Administration
and later on to the International Refugee Organization. I worked as
welfare and education officer in five displaced persons camps and
Jewish communities in small towns. One of my responsibilities was to
work for the resettlement of the Jewish displaced persons in Palestine.
A few months after the establishment of the Jewish state, I was assigned to work as a transport officer accompanying thousands of displaced persons from Germany to Marseille on their way to Israel.
Twenty-one months after I had left Jerusalem, I returned there to the
position of a school social worker. Together with one other worker, I
set up the beginning program of school social work in the city of
Jerusalem.

I came to the United States to learn because I knew that I was lacking many things. I wanted to continue to work in social work and I
recognized my need for formal training badly. I had often thought of
the United States and the opportunities it presented because I had
had contact with American social workers and Israeli social workers
who had their training in America.

The student who comes to America comes with certain ideas about
it, for America is still a magic word for many people. These ideas
come from the Hollywood movie, from American novels he has read,
from Americans he has met abroad, from his countrymen who have
visited America and from the newspapers at home.

Plenty and Guilt

The foreign student, who comes to the United States from a land
where food and other necessities are rationed, is thrust suddenly into a
land of plenty. He is overwhelmed by the plenty and is guilty that he
has so much to eat and in such great variety, while his people at home
must do without. He is jealous that this country has so much and that
this country is whole while his homeland has so little and has been
broken by war. He sees that this country is so large and his country is
so small. This feeling of jealousy he has to deny to himself, as jealousy
is not "nice" and not a proper emotion for an intelligent adult. He may
see the many comforts people have, their high standard of living, the
cars, the washing machines, the refrigerators, etc. He envies what

seems to him an easy life and wishes that it were so in his own land. On the other hand, he feels resentment and bewilderment at the tremendous waste which he sees around him. The waste, the plenty, and his denial of his jealousy increase his resentment not only to the school and to the people who teach him, but to the American way of life in general. It seems to him that they are unaware of the world outside, and that they do not know what life is really like. They have been sheltered, they have not experienced the fear and hunger he has known, and to him it must seem that they have little or no curiosity or interest in how others in the world live and die.

Only later does he realize how incomprehensible war and its destruction may be to those who have not experienced it. Only later it occurs to him that behind this unwillingness to know may lie guilt and defense.

Meanwhile he finds himself reacting to the plenty and defending himself against it. He tries to work out guilt feelings by hoarding newspapers in his room to use as wrapping paper, as this may have been his pattern for years or it may be that despite the paper rationing at home, he had never been able to be so saving before. During my first 3 weeks in America for the first time in my life I saved every scrap of paper. I saw the waste around me and remembered that at home paper is difficult to get; besides, there was the fear that all this might disappear tomorrow.

The student cannot throw food away; he has seen people hungry and receives letters from home that there is not enough to eat. And so he has to eat the old bread before he can buy a fresh loaf of bread. To throw away the stale bread would increase his guilt even more that he has enough to eat.

The student also looks ahead to the return home, wanting this return and fearing it. And so he must continue to deny to himself the good and the pleasant and what he sees as the value in the American way of life in order not to be involved too much to be free for that return. Several students have told me that they held back from making friends because in 2 years they would leave anyhow. Sometimes because of this denial and this fear he may hide behind an air of arrogance and indifference and condemn himself to solitude, thus denying himself fullest use of the experience which is his.

It is inevitable that the student is much involved and concerned with what is going on in his own land. When he opens an American newspaper he has to see first if there is anything written about his own country.. Mail is awaited impatiently, as this is the means whereby he maintains his all-important contact with home. One of the students I knew had to run home regularly to see if he had mail instead of joining the other students in their leisure activities. It seems to me that he did this not only because he felt lonely, but perhaps also he felt guilty about being here at all. He had therefore to restrict himself, to miss out on making new friends and thus overcoming his loneliness. He could not bear to make full use of his stay in this country.

And there are the many things which are done differently in the U.S.A. than they are at home. When the student buys a Sunday paper it seems to him that he is walking off with the whole newsstand, for at home his Sunday paper has only 4 to 6 pages.

The Barrier of Language

Together with all this he experiences language difficulties and this when language is his major means of communication. I can say it in Hebrew, in German and in Yiddish but the right word at the moment I need it I can find nowhere in the English language. He is cut off from familiar customs and ties and so even when there is no serious language problem, he is ill at ease with the foreign language and its colloquial expressions and idioms, and this further increases his feelings of being an outsider.

Anger and resistance may grow too in reaction to the often-encountered attitude that everything in America is the best and biggest and greatest and in the reaction to what often appears to be a complete absence of curiosity regarding the student's own country.

Amid all this conflict of impressions and feelings and thoughts, he is thrown at once into school and work, sometimes after he has been in the United States for a few days and sometimes right from the airplane when the semester has already started.

Returning to the role of a student in a school for social work with its strict curriculum, required courses and class attendance represents for him consciously or unconsciously a loss of status. To be a student in a social agency setting where previously he had enjoyed an equal rank with other workers is not an easy transition. He doubts his own skills and wonders what kinds of relationship he will have. He has to learn the way of the new agency and community. The things he was accustomed to do, because he knew the setting, are now strange to him and he has to depend on others.

As I said above, I came to the United States with the will to learn because I knew and felt that I was lacking many things. I felt that I could not continue to work without getting further training. At the same time I wondered and in the beginning did not allow myself to question what "they" would be able to teach me. Part of me wanted to learn and part of me resisted the learning without being aware of it. I was afraid of the new experience and wondered how I would make out. Would I be able to sit after so many years and study and write papers? Will I do well and not disappoint those who gave me the opportunity to study? I also had expectations of myself and wanted to make the most of this experience. The whole process of separation and my coming here, my hopes and my fears involved so much that I felt that the result must be something of equal significance.

In consequence, from the beginning I put myself under great pressure. From the very first I started to evaluate all my interviews not only in terms of the dynamics and diagnoses, but also in terms of techniques. I pressed my supervisor very hard to do the same. For a short while she did until she realized how threatening this kind of pointing out the lacks in my skills and knowledge was to me. She refused to continue and then her refusal became even more threatening to me. At this point we had some stormy supervisory sessions until I was able to work through my feelings and understand. It is difficult to have one's inadequacy confirmed by another. I felt my own inadequacies and knowing them I would have liked rather to find them myself and to know the answers instead of having them pointed out. I was already questioning myself, my inadequacy and my competence. I had to project my feelings on those who taught me and for quite a while I felt myself continually under attack.

The student has high expectations of those who are teaching him, and makes great demands of them without being aware of it. Perhaps the loss of status he feels in being a student again brings some regression in it and dependency. And he struggles against dependency. On the one hand he has high demands and expectations from others, and yet at the same time he must devaluate.

Attitudes of Teachers

In this new experience which involves cultural differences and a working through of his feelings related to taking on a new role, to meeting expectations of himself and of others, what are the attitudes in those who teach him which deepen his resistance to learning, and what are the attitudes which are most helpful in bringing about his adjustment? The student may meet with lack of knowledge in regard to what is going on in his own country, particularly in the field of social work. This again raises the question of how much can "they" teach him and what will he be able to use when he goes back, and how can "they" know which courses or which field placement will best meet his needs.

If we accept that a caseworker must be acquainted with the cultural background of the client, is it not valid to expect that the supervisors and teachers should be acquainted with the cultural background of their students? Is it helpful that a student may have completed his graduate work and find that during these 2 years his two advisors and two supervisors never once have asked how he was able to use what he brought with him? The student who told me this adjusted well to the reality, but there was a tone of resentment in giving me this account. After she was graduated and a few days before she left, by chance in a casual meeting, this question was put to her by a supervisor from another agency. If it had not been for this casual meeting, she would have left America without ever hearing the question; "What did you bring with you?" Other students have told me of similar experiences and one wonders why the student's experience is completely brushed aside. Is it that the supervisor is threatened by the student's experience and therefore cannot ask about it? Is it that the past experience is not considered valuable? Is it that the supervisor assumes that the student is going to learn everything in America?

Perhaps acknowledging the student's experiences instead of brushing them aside, acknowledging that because of his experiences he is here and the skills he has shown thus far, would be helpful and would free him to question himself and his past and make it easier for him to go on learning. I am not a supervisor and so far I have not read a single book on supervision, but my past formal training was in teaching and it seems to me that this is one of the basic principles of teaching—that we build on what the student brings.

There is no doubt that casework training by its very nature involves anxieties for all students, and more particularly for the experienced one who has worked before. Now it seems to him that he has lost all his skills and he is involved in the difficult process of new learning and unlearning. He has the problem of the centipede who could walk all his life until he was asked "which foot comes after which." Then he could not walk anymore. This is the insecurity and the struggle with new concepts, new ideas, more theoretical knowledge, and newly acquired skills that are not yet integrated. This struggle and insecurity are also related to the student's feeling of loss of status with his questioning of his past experience, with the continuous examination of self which is so necessarily a part of learning. The student has the need to refer to his past experience. This is not only a defense. He has to review the past in order to integrate the new knowledge. He has to challenge the new ideas in order to integrate them. The need to evaluate is also related to the fact that despite the pressure of classwork and fieldwork, he has more time to think than he had before and perhaps will ever have again, and also to the stimulation from his present work and his classroom learning.

The Question of Use

Is this a denial of what is going on in social work in other countries, is it a lack of curiosity, or is it that the feeling that only America has something to teach, that the only and eternal question the foreign student ever hears is "How will you use what you have learned in America"? When this is the only question the student ever hears and not also "How could you use what you brought with you," how can he be helped to think in terms of applying what he has learned in America in his homeland? And ought this not be done? since the student before his return must and wants to a much greater extent than before to shift the focus to what he is going to do when he returns home; what to use and how to use it. Surely the main responsibility is upon the student and in 2 years conditions in his country might have changed. But is this not to a certain part the responsibility of his teachers to help him with it? But how can they help him when they never got acquainted with what is awaiting the student.

When on the other hand the student finds interest expressed in his country, he is thereby helped to overcome his resistance.

I do not want to overgeneralize from my experience. But from the little I know and observed and listened to, it seems to me that some of what I experienced was not unique. Others too had had to struggle with it, because each of us has something in common with his fellow man. But I know from my own experience that I shall never forget my first interview, in which my advisor showed me a pamphlet about a certain field of social work in Israel, or that my supervisor greeted me with the remark that she was just reading a book about my country and asked me for a list of other books. I think that both incidents, occurring as they did in the first days of my American experience, helped me in the long run to lessen the feeling of loneliness, which I was then trying not very successfully to deny to myself. The fact that my advisor and supervisor knew something about Israel and drew me out to tell what I did so far gave me, among all the confusion, some security. Working through all this and more and learning to recognize and, to a certain degree, to handle my defense have helped me to learn.

There are foreign students who are called "exchange students" who come to the United States to study and to learn about America in general and also to give Americans better understanding of what is going on in their own countries in general and in the profession. It seems to me that partly because of this the program and the term "exchange" has been developed. The American government, private agencies, the United Nations and others spend money on exchange students who are brought to this country. From the United States social workers travel to other countries, to conferences, to work and to observe. But while foreign students are here—and among them many who are qualified—often no use is made of them either by the school or by the profession in general. Where are the teachers and the professionals in general who make use of this "exchange" and try to take advantage of it? (Very often it seems as if the other students are the only ones who want to know.) Where is the professional curiosity which usually seems to be so characteristic of social workers? Somehow, in spite of all the money spent or the words spoken about it, the idea of exchange is lost somewhere along the way.

Perhaps an American social worker is better qualified to understand the reason for the loss. To many with whom I spoke it seemed that this lack of curiosity is a defense. Others see in it the attitude that Americans think that they know everything better and that they do not have to learn anything and that only what is learned in America is of importance.

The question "How will you use what you learned?" is pertinent and valid. But valid too would be "What have you brought?" In this is the real essence of "exchange" which the program of foreign students makes possible.

Holocaust Survivors and Their Children

This paper addresses itself to work with the survivors of the holocaust and their children, those who escaped concentration camps and ghettos, who spent life hiding in forests, cellars and cloisters, or living on Aryan identification papers. It addresses itself to the attitude of the helping professions in facing the survivor, the event of the holocaust itself, and the survivor's frequent unwillingness to accept professional help.

The Jewish community has given generously to the survivors, but more often than not we have been unable to help them with their emotional problems of living. We know that war, disasters, immigration, create problems that have a generational effect. This is all the more true for the survivors of the holocaust, who were exposed to extraordinary circumstances. The new immigrants who are arriving now at our shores force us all the more to be alert to their emotional needs.

The problem of what to do with these forsaken, almost lost souls is immense but one which, if not tackled and solved, will make all our efforts a mere waste of time, for then it were kinder to have let them die than to have brought them back

---

Reprinted with permission from Norman Linzer, The Jewish Family, second edition, (New York: Federation of Jewish Philanthropies, 1970).

to mere existence and more suffering in a hostile world, where they no longer have even a hope of being able to compete in the struggle of the survival of the fittest and must inevitably go down.[1]

Twenty-five years later, we still witness an unwillingness to discuss the holocaust by many of our clients and their workers. This is so despite the fact that today we often are called upon to help the traumatized children and grandchildren, the third generation of these forsaken, "almost lost souls." Everyone who has worked with the survivors of the holocaust knows that many of them are reluctant to seek and use help. The reasons for this reluctance are manifold: for some, going for help might mean acknowledging that the Germans were right in their judgment about the Jews as damaged, inferior people; for some it might mean acknowledging that the Germans succeeded in damaging them and turning them into inferior people forever; others cannot accept help because it means to them giving up the feeling of omnipotence, of being superior because they "willed" to survive. The feeling of guilt for having survived while others died is always present, as is often the feeling of shame for having "betrayed" and "allowed" fathers, siblings, wife or children to die. That guilt or shame can hold one back from entering a treatment relationship is known to all of us. Another complication is the fact that many survivors have lost the capacity to trust and to enter into a relationship. They feel themselves isolated from the world around them, and feel that their horrible experience has set them apart from the rest of the world forever. All of us know survivors who have never even told their children about their life during the holocaust.

Nevertheless it has been my experience that the client's "mentioning" having been in concentration camp is not picked up, an impression that is borne out by Dr. Niederland's [2] observations of the helping professions. It is my guess that it is the rare worker who picks up on the concentration camp experience and helps parents and their children to deal with this trauma and its consequences.

The event itself exposes our inability to comprehend and understand, to come to terms with, to listen to what life in a concentration camp meant, such as being exposed every minute of the day and the night, lining up in front of gas chambers, seeing human beings turned into material. Thus we miss clues that ordinarily we would pick up on. "I was in Bergen Belsen and you cannot understand this," says the client. "No, I cannot understand," says the worker, thereby shutting the client off forever. This statement either increases the client's resistance that was there to begin with, or fosters the part that does not want to tell. Instead, the worker could address himself to the positive side of the client's ambivalence, the part which wants to speak, by responding, "Tell me so that I can understand."

Although we acknowledge in "ordinary" cases that extreme traumas, such as natural disasters, war or slavery, leave their ongoing imprint on the personality and affect adjustment to life and parenthood, we do not seem to acknowledge the far-reaching generational effects of the events of the holocaust, even on those yet unborn. Yet we do see them inflicted upon generations yet unborn, generations that often will not know that this period existed.

The effect on many of the survivors of the holocaust has been defined as the survivor or concentration camp syndrome; it consists of psychic or somatic symptoms and various manifestations. It is complex in its nature; past danger is felt as present danger, chronic depression, apathy, detachment, permanent feeling of loss, insomnia, partial or complete amnesia, character changes.[3] Therefore, the survivor syndrome must have had an influence on these clients and their children. But it goes unrecognized and ignored in the treatment process.

Case Illustrations

The following verbatim quotation from one of my cases will help to highlight the point.

CASE A

"What will I tell my child when she will ask me who were my parents, what were their names, what did they look like?"

It was utterly in despair at the point where Mrs. D. herself became a mother. She herself was found, together with other children, in 1945, roaming the streets of a European town. She was 2¼ years old. Nobody ever claimed her. Her question highlights the feeling of being faceless and points to her unresolved identity.

Discussion

Although this young woman has made a reasonable adjustment, there is the danger that motherhood will reawaken her trauma of having lost her mother in infancy. Her tendency toward depression makes pregnancy and feeding especially dangerous times for her. As her child becomes older there is the danger that the nightmare will now include her child. This is documented by Krystal, Neiderland [4] and others who found that their adult survivors frequently included in their persecution dreams their children who were not yet born at the time of their persecution by the Nazis. They report that these patients have compulsive obsessions about injury to their children. It is thus self-evident that the survivor syndrome does not consist of fixed symptoms, but can take on additional symptoms because of new circumstances or new crises. This is not to imply that concentration camp victims have never been able to overcome the trauma by themselves, or with professional help, but it implies that in time of crisis—external or developmental—the old trauma can be reawakened and professional help will be needed and should be available. But to help, the professional has to be alert to these possibilities, the danger of regression under pressure.

In order to be of help, the professional has to know and understand the historic reality of the holocaust, and his own attitude toward this event.

Knowledge about the holocaust is important in order not to perpetuate negative myths about the victims. We and our children are angry and judgmental, asking "why did Jews allow themselves to go to slaughter like cattle, without fighting?" The Eichmann trial changed this image for Israeli youth, but it did not do so here. There are few who realize that Jewish resistance arose not only in the Warsaw ghetto, but also in Treblinka, Sobibor, Auschwitz and Platzow. [5] They do not realize that many, even if they wanted to escape, had no place to go. The United States and other countries had closed their gates. If they escaped, partisans often turned them in, since the partisans had one thing in common with the Nazis—the solution of the Jewish problem.

Youth does not know that even in ghettoes and camps Jews tried to keep school for children. They do not know that Jews tried to escape and emigrate, but knocked on closed doors; Jews bought entry permits to various countries for a great deal of money—permits that were not worth the paper on which they were printed. They tried to escape by land and by sea to Israel, then Palestine, through "illegal" *Aliyah.* Our youth does not know about the "illegal" refugee ship, the "Struma," which sank with all its fleeing passengers in the Black Sea in 1942.

Above all, who can really understand the day-to-day humiliation, degradation, physical and psychological assault? The ever-present danger of death literally from one minute to another had no rhyme or reason and, even if one survived once, there was no guarantee that he would survive the next minute, hour, night or day.

We seem to be more familiar with Arendt's "The Banality of Evil" and Bettelheim's "Anna Frank Family" than with "Babi Yaar" or "The Last of the Just" or the documents and writings that have come from Yad Vashem.* In other words, the victim is as guilty as the victimizer. Youth does not understand that the Jews went to the gas chambers because of the sins of commission and omission of the world around them. Or, as so aptly stated by Bychowsky: "A number of very gifted . . . individuals like Victor Frankl . . . survived. . . . Can we demand this from everybody? Have people been created by God to have special courage . . . ?" [6]

To this I would want to add the question, without in any way minimizing people like Frankl who were able to maintain a great moral strength "without even surrendering to the guards": Could they have survived if the war would have continued? Do we not all have a breaking point? Could it be that survival was also a matter of luck, that survival did not necessarily depend on being exceptional? What of the exceptional courage shown by those who chose to go to their death rather than desert those they loved or were responsible for? Such a one was Janus Korczak [7] who chose to accompany the children of the Warsaw Jewish Orphanage of which he was director, rather than to take advantage of opportunities offered to him for escape.

Another myth—the opposite of the one that if you would have wanted to, you could have survived—is that in order to survive, the

---

* Freely translated as: Israeli Holocaust Remembrance Authority.

victim must have collaborated, and sacrificed others to buy his life. Thus we have incorporated the world's negative view about Jews, and have transmitted it to our children. In our work, then, the survivor senses our negative attitude, or countertransference, which he has incorporated. He feels himself judged by us, is reluctant to talk and cannot confide in us. Since we know about countertransference, are we surprised that the concentration camp victims are often "uncooperative cases"?

The holocaust highlights the victimizer's loss of the last trace of humaneness and human dignity, and demonstrates that man can be his own most dangerous weapon. It was, and for many still is, a nightmare that we would like to believe has never happened, or to forget completely. "It cannot be true," therefore it could not have happened. It was an event impossible to encompass or to understand. Man's inhumanity to his fellow man can easily lead to despair and hopelessness about man, were it not for the fact that the victims are a symbol of man's capacity to preserve his dignity and his humanity, even at unbelievably high cost to himself.

The Language of Explanation

There is no frame of reference that could explain what the Nazis did, be it in historical, psychological, religious, political, economic, philosophical or fictional writing. The language to explain the unparalleled disaster does not yet exist and our terminology to understand the survivor is deficient. Thus, while the psychiatric literature uses for the survivors terms such as "traumatic neurosis," "defense," and "the concept of trauma," there are some professionals who question the adequacy of the terms for those extraordinary circumstances.

Language can be a dangerous weapon if used inappropriately. It can hide and cover up deeds, and distract people from understanding what is happening to them. The Germans were masters in the way they used language to mislead their own population, the Jews and the Allies. Ghettoes often were called residential areas. Concentration camps were called resettlements. "Final solution" was a euphemism for murder of the Jews.

Yet the effort to probe, understand, explain and reconstruct the psychological and physical effect upon the survivor during and after the holocaust is admirable, since it highlights man's wish to understand. Sometimes these efforts, expressed in various psychological, physiological, sociological and historical frames of reference, highlight the humaneness of the professionals as well as their limitations. A paper like "Studies of Concentration Camp Survivors," [8] which highlights the assault on the personality, exploring in depth the systematic assault on the victim step by step, day by day, the Musulman stage (a stage of complete apathy, a living corpse), can help us to be aware intellectually and perhaps emotionally of what the concentration camp was like.

It is hard or perhaps impossible to keep one's scientific detachment. At times one deals with human beings so fragile that their recall of this period can make for further breakdown of their personality. Often, especially in short-term treatment, our goals have to be limited, and all that the professional can do is to help the survivor to live with his memories. We know that some of the victims are unable to recall what happened to them, as they suffer from partial or complete amnesia. Whether this is due to psychic or somatic reasons is often impossible to establish. There are those who ascribe it to psychic sources—that the victim has to defend himself against memories that would be overwhelming for him. There are others who think that the constant beating on the head to which victims were exposed resulted in brain damage.[9, 10] It is astonishing that there are so few people who turned into psychopaths after having to endure what we cannot conceive in our wildest imagination.

Again, this is not to imply that all survivors need professional help. There are those who seem to have found their place among us, and at times we are surprised when we learn that they are survivors. There are those who have become successful in their professions or vocations, but when it comes to the enjoyment of life or forming meaningful relationships and good marriages they are unable to do so. Basic trust seems to be missing. There are those burdened with guilt, who just seem to exist rather than live.

CASE B

Mrs. A., close to 40, divorced after 1 year of marriage, and her mother are the only ones who survived of a nuclear family of four. Her sister, the mother's favorite, was deported on Mrs. A's birthday. She, who was the sickly, the ugly one, survived. On her birthday her mother made her light a memorial candle for the deceased sister.

Discussion

For Mrs. A. her birthday is a day of mourning, and she blames herself for having survived while her sister, the favorite, was led to slaughter. Mrs. A.'s childish wish to have her sister out of the way so that she could be the only beloved daughter became cruel reality. She remained arrested at an infantile level of magical thinking.

Case C

The B.s came to this country in their early 20s. Their life is circumscribed. They have no friends; life is full of danger and somatic complaints. They fear for the life of their son, who is a delinquent, but it is the world who wants to hurt and destroy him.

Discussion

Unconsciously, the B.s have allowed their son to act out their own highly repressed aggressive feelings against the world, a world that is bad and dangerous. In other words, we see that parents allow their children to do what was dangerous for them to do. They had to hold in and repress their aggression in order to survive. There are others who will call this kind of son a Nazi or a Hitler and one almost feels an identification and an admiration with the aggressor. There are others for whom the children represent the lost member of their families. There are children who know of their parents' life during the war. They have heard hints here and there and have lived with their parents' chronic depression. They go around feeling burdened, feeling that they have to make up for their parents' suffering. This wish to make up at times expresses itself by putting high demands for achievement upon themselves, scholastic and/or material. In this effort they often refuse their parents' help or accept it, feeling guilty while doing so.

In all these cases we have to reach out to the parents and help them to discuss their experiences with their children. If they cannot do so, we have to do it. Possibly the children will gain understanding and empathy, seeing how and why their parents relate to them as they do. Perhaps this will help to break the generational effect.

We know that those who were children or adolescents during the holocaust were one of the most damaged groups. Not all were able to take hold of what Eisler calls "the second chance of adolescence."

CASE D

Miss C.'s only memory of her parents is that they had put her in a cupboard together with her girl friend and that they were told not to cry. If they would cry the Nazis would come and take them away. She, age 3, cried, and the Nazis came and her parents disappeared in a big stove, the gas chamber.

Discussion

For Miss C., with the disappearance of her parents, a phantasy common to all children, her worst wishes and desires became a harsh reality. That is a fact we always have to remember in working with those survivors who were children or adolescents when they lost their parents.

CASE E

Mr. R. left his parents and his sister against their will to emigrate to Israel with the illegal *aliyah* in the 30s. He was 16 then and as long as there was still the possibility to write to Germany, he kept begging them to join him in Israel. His parents and sisters were killed in the gas chambers. He has refused any reparation money and has undergone many financial hardships, preferring to do manual labor instead of following his desires and talents academically. He says if he had stayed with them, he might have saved them.

Discussion

Some survivors have refused German reparation money until today, at times preferring to struggle financially instead of accepting what they call "blood money." "I cannot be bought off." "I shall not release the Germans from their deeds." I have heard this expressed at times. Others have taken reparation money, at times quoting the Prophet Elijah, who, approaching King Achav after he killed the owner of the vineyard he desired, said: "You killed and you want to inherit too. No, says the Lord."

Others of my clients who lost their parents in early childhood have accepted reparation money, after initial refusal, in the course of therapy. There is no question that the refusal of reparations from the German government, as well as the acceptance of reparations, is highly overdetermined and complex in its nature. Yet whatever the clients' conscious or unconscious motivation, we have to respect their decision. Often all that we can do, especially in short-term therapy, is to help them to live in peace with their decision.

CASE F[11]

Mr. and Mrs. Z., while in a concentration camp, lost one child and gave birth to a second. In the U.S. they could not cope with the girl's wild behavior, and sent her to a boarding school. Then they urged her into a teen-age marriage. The marriage lasted just long enough to produce a son, at which time the daughter separated from her husband to rejoin her parents. The daughter, never having experienced mothering, is chronically depressed and threatens suicide. She is self-indulgent in her behavior and cannot be a mother to her son. He has learning difficulties, is hyperactive, aggressive and destructive.

Discussion

Danto's discussion of "the role of the missed adolescence," E. Streba's [13] and Anna Freud's [14] and others' [15, 16] work on children and adolescents of the holocaust highlight the danger of generational effect. Kaboff, like others, points to the ever-present danger of suicide in these victims, and states: "We must have been idiots to think that the effect of the terrible experience would not be passed on to future generations." [17]

I have seen a number of survivors who lost their parents in early childhood and were apparently symptom-free until adolescence. The same has been reported by others and also about adult survivors.

There are survivors who have never been able to work through their grief and mourning. For years many have kept on searching for their relatives; they do not know where they were buried, almost all have no graves to visit, and they do not know the date of Yahrzeit. Some even today have not accepted that their relatives are really dead. That for years after the holocaust missed relatives still turned up perhaps contributed to these phantasies.

Jacob, who delayed working because of mourning, is an example of an individual's inability to believe that his parents died.

CASE G

Jacob lost his parents when he was 16. He was then living in Israel. They had stayed behind in Europe, hoping to join him after taking care of their business affairs. Twenty years later, when his only surviving uncle died, he had to see the dead body again and again. It was obvious that he did not believe that his uncle had died and it was only after he had accepted the death of his uncle that he started to accept the death of his parents.

The holocaust has been the most horrendous experience mankind has ever witnessed. Those who survived are an atypical group—atypical since the large majority exposed to the holocaust perished. It does not become us to ask "How come you survived?" or "How come you don't trust us?," or "How come 25 years later the world still looks like Hitler's world to you?" It is for us to marvel that the survivor still goes on living and has remained human, feeling guilty and suffering. The Nazis lost these human emotions; the survivors retained them. The survivor is thus a living witness to the dignity of man.

References

1. D. Collins W.K.F. "Belsen Camp," Brit. Med. J.F 1945, pp. 814-816, quoted in L. Eitinger, Concentration Camp, Seminars in Norway and Israel, Oslo-London Universitetsparlatet, 1964.
2. Henry Krystal (ed.) Massive Psychic Trauma, New York: International Universities Press, Inc., 1968.
3. W. G. Niederland, "An Interpretation of the Psychological Stresses and Defense: Concentration Camp Life and the Late After-effect," Ibid., pp. 60-70. Therese Beyenek, "Parenthood as a Developmental Phase: A Contribu-

tion to the Libido Theory," Journal of the American Psychoanalytic Association, Vol. 7, July, 1959, pp. 384-417.
4. Krystal, op. cit., p. 330.
5. Nora Levin. The Holocaust: The Destruction of European Jewry, 1933-1945, New York: Thomas Y. Crowell Company, 1968.
6. Krystal, op. cit., p. 103.
7. Selected Works of Janus Z. Korczak. Published for the National Science Foundation, Washington, D.C. by the Scientific Publications, Foreign Cooperation Center of the Central Institute for Scientific, Technical and Economic Information on Warsaw, Poland, 1967.
8. Krystal, op. cit., pp. 24-47.
9. Eitinger, op. cit.
10. G. Bychowski, "Permanent Character Changes as an After-Effect of Persecution." Krystal, op. cit., pp. 75-87.
11. From a case presented by Mr. Pincher Berger, student in my casework class at Wurzweiler School of Social Work, Yeshiva University.
12. Bruce L. Danto, "The Role of Missed Adolescence in the Etiology of the Concentration Camp Survivor Syndrome," Krystal, op. cit., pp. 248-277.
13. Edith Streba, "The Effect of Persecution on Adolescents." Ibid., pp. 51-60.
14. Anna Freud and S. Dann. "An Experiment in Group Upbringing," The Psychoanalytic Study of the Child, New York: International Universities Press, Vol. 6, 1951, pp. 127-168.
15. E. L. Gyomnoi. "The Analysis of a Young Concentration Camp Victim," The Psychoanalytic Study of the Child, Vol. 18, New York: International Universities Press, 1963, pp. 484-510.
16. Edith Streba, "Emotional Problems of Displaced Children, Casework, Vol. 30, 1949, pp. 175-181.
17. Jewish Chronicle, 1969.
18. Niederland. "As important as early factors for the pathogenic manifestations of neurotic and psychotic conditions are, they can never be the sole consideration in the psychiatric evaluation of verbal disorders in concentration camp survivors." Krystal, op. cit., pp. 11-12. See also paper by Hillel Klein, "Problems in the Psychological Treatment of Israeli Survivors of the Holocaust," Ibid., p. 233.
19. Ibid., p. 15.

Introduction

Israel has been characterized as having a child-centered culture. The loss of so many Jewish lives from the holocaust and the persecutions in Mideast countries made each new life precious to the budding country. This was reflected in the outstanding network of schools, institutions, kibbutz placements, and other child welfare services developed by Youth Aliyah during and after the holocaust. Child psychologists, educators and psychiatrists from all over were enlisted in setting up these services. It was in Israel that Gerald Caplan devised some of his early theories on mental health consultation. The actual caretakers were often not professionally trained, and a framework was sought to help them utilize the services of the high-level professionals. The Appelberg article on consultation, in this section, contains almost all of the basic theories of the consulting process.

Because of a socialist philosophy and a Zionist idealism, placement of children in Israel in child-centered settings was seen as a major option. There was a tendency to minimize the extent of pathology in the belief that placement in a democratic setting with good facilities would in itself be therapeutic. In the years since these articles, public agencies as well as Youth Aliyah have developed a broad range of alternatives to institutionalization (foster homes, day care, etc.) Many parents, children of immigrants discussed in these articles, still feel, however, that their children would have a better opportunity for growth away from home.

Esther Appelberg's vision of child welfare was one of combined sophistication, awareness of social and cultural trends, and a pragmatic ability to deal with the realities of agencies and staff. Today, care of children in their own homes and family treatment are beginning to be considered in child care plans, suggestions that Dr. Appelberg made years ago. The dilemma of the child welfare worker . . . to accept the child without rejecting the parent—in fact, to help the parent with his feelings of inadequacy, to help him be a better parent without losing identification with the child and his needs—this is the essence of Dr. Appelberg's philosophy as illustrated in these articles.

Naomi Abramowitz
Ramat Gan, Israel

The Request for Child Placement in Israel

This paper describes my experience as area supervisor in the field of child welfare in a public agency. This area of work included, among others, an old township, well established agricultural settlements, new collective agricultural settlements and maabaroth. In general, the paper * concerns itself with the oriental population of this area.

I shall describe the problems involved in requests for placement of children, especially young ones, in terms of the following factors: a) the interplay between the cultural and personal motivation of the parents in their request for placement of their children as influenced by the Israeli scene; b) the cultural as well as emotional motivation of the social worker in dealing with the request; c) the motivations of parents and workers with regard to placement that seem to be universal. Recommendations are made for dealing with these problems.

Israel is a pioneer country whose early settlers were people coming

Reprinted with permission from the Journal of Jewish Communal Service, XXXIII, 4, Summer 1957.
* For part of the case material I am indebted to my colleagues and my supervisees with whom I worked for a year and a half. I also wish to thank Dr. Helen Faigin, research psychologist of the Lasker Mental Hygiene and Child Guidance Center of Hadassah, Jerusalem, for her invaluable suggestions and advice regarding the form and style of this paper.

mainly .from Europe in the early years of the 20th century. These settlers broke their ties with their parents, left their homes and country to establish a new society. They wished to establish a different and better world from the one in which they had grown up. Thus the eternal conflict between parents and sons was a participating factor in helping the Zionist movement. Zionism used political parties and youth movements to recruit members. Through these parties, youth movements and agricultural training centers they tried to educate young people to a new set of values, strongly influenced by socialistic ideals.

Youth Aliyah,** which was created in the 30s, for the purpose of rescuing children from Europe and to a lesser extent also from other countries, adopted the method of group care. Its first wards were parentless children or children whose parents stayed behind. An important factor in sending children away from home to Israel was, of course, the persecution of the Jews. Parents who still hoped they could manage in Europe wanted to make sure that their children, at least, would be safe. Others knew that they themselves could not save their lives but that the child could be saved. From the British Mandate to the present time parents have sent their children to Israel in the hope that this would help them to get into the country on a priority basis. Some parents, both among Oriental Jews and Jews from European countries and Latin America, sent their children to Israel because they could not manage them at home. Oriental Jews sometimes send their children due to economic difficulties and under the influence of "Shlichim" (emissaries). The method of group care was selected because Youth Aliyah's aim was not only to help the children adjust to a certain social reality, but to further the social ideal of joining a collective settlement and living in a collective framework. In other words, Youth Aliyah was a movement that had an educational ideal wherein national needs take precedence over the needs of the individual. Through its education Youth Aliyah tried to utilize the conflict be-

---

** (Editor's note: Youth Aliyah continues to be an outstanding agency for the education and care of children in Israel. Patterns of immigration and needs for care have changed. Consequently the population served by Youth Aliyah and the services offered have shifted. Today the agency provides for children from deprived backgrounds whether or not they are new immigrants. A broad range of educational and placement services has been developed.)

tween the generations to bring the pupils to identify with the ideal of collective life rather than the individualistic life of their parents.

Idealism as Factor

Parents in Israel send their children to institutions not only because of broken marriages and other social conditions, but because they too believe in the ideal of the collective environment. At least for German youth, a children's village in Israel like Ben-Shemen had a certain romanticism and was influenced by the "Landschulheim." The children pressed their elders to go to Israel just as children in Israel pressed their elders to let them join the kibbutz. Here again we see how the adolescent finds an outlet through Zionism in his struggle with his parents. So we see that even though the founders were small in numbers and got smaller because of the big immigration that did not bring the same idealistic elements, their influence was very strong. A positive element inherent in the competition of the various parties to gain future members is that the newcomer has the same chance as the old-timer in belonging to one of the groups, and admittance to the established society is open to him.

With Israel's view to the future, children became important, since they were the hope of the future, the ones to realize the dreams of their elders. It is therefore understandable that this society became to a large extent a child-centered one, and child care in Israel developed much earlier and to a greater extent than care for the aged.

One of the outstanding trends in child care has been the setting up of closed institutions for all ages by all political parties and women's organizations. These institutions provide care for infants, toddlers, school children and adolescents. Nearly all of them are set up to care for the "average, normal" child. The kibbutzim have also started to accept the "average, normal" child on an individual basis in order to be able to have enough children to provide teaching for their own. All of them have a special boarding rate for children who are referred by the social agency, and the rate is much lower than the actual cost. This agreement between the organizations and the social agency thus works two ways, since the former want to accept a child and ask the social agency to participate in the cost. Society sees the child's place at home, but society also sees the child's place away from home when it thinks that the parent does not fulfill his obligations. Every social worker is familiar with the request of schools, neighbors, rabbis and volunteer organizations to place a child away from home when his parents do not bring him up properly. So the public agency is asked to pay for a child who has been placed in an institution by one of the volunteer organizations or political parties.

Here is a case in point: Mr. B came to the agency asking them to pay for RB, a 10-year-old girl who had been placed by him in one of the institutions operated by his political party. He had found the girl strolling near the mission school, playing truant. She had been brought to his attention by the neighbor, who also complained about her stealing. He had convinced her parents that they were unable to educate their child. As the parents were unable to participate in the payment for the girl, he wanted the public agency to help his institution in the upkeep of the child.

The social worker was much surprised, since he knew the family. Some of the problems the girl presented had been discussed with her mother, but the question of placement had never arisen. In the interview with the parents he discovered that they, too, had been confronted with a *fait accompli*. This case illustrates that we have to take into consideration not only the emotional conflict and makeup of the parent, but the cultural climate, namely, that institutions are good for children because either the parents or the children are "bad."

Foster home care and group care in families are developed to a negligible degree.* In 1954 we had 0.42% of all the children who are not in their own homes in foster homes, and 1.06% in family group homes. Those small percentages are attributable not only to low and late payment of board and crowded living conditions that make it difficult to accept children for board, but to the philosophy that sees the institution as a better place for the child who has to be reared outside his own home. It is also worth mentioning that a large percentage of the children boarded in foster families are the exceptional ones, the defective ones for whom no institutional care could be found

---

* Since this article was written, foster care programs have been developed in public agencies in Israel. Nevertheless, institutional placement remains the major option.

and who often might have been better off if a suitable institution had been available for them. There were 3.74% of the child population in the age group 0-18 reared outside their own homes in 1949.

Wide Differences

When we turn our attention to the Oriental Jews, the new immigrants, we have to realize that the differences among the various groups are great and manifold. There is not only a difference between the Yemenite Jew from South Arabia, and the Moroccan Jew from Casablanca, but great variation within each group, depending on the area from which they come—city or isolated village. We also have to realize that we know little about their way of life. The little we have observed about their mores and patterns of culture has not been observed in their country of origin, but in Israel. Therefore often the patterns of behavior observed have already undergone change and disruption because of contact with Israel and the necessity to adapt to a changing world. Nonetheless, there are certain generalizations we can make. Some of the patterns of behavior are reactions to the new surroundings, not necessarily particular to the Oriental Jew in Israel, but found also among the European Jews. The problem of adaptation and the difficulties involved are common to all groups of immigrants, wherever they may find themselves.

The old-timers and their leaders came for the most part with a positive outlook toward Israel, a wish to establish a new society and to achieve a total transformation of their way of life. They began to prepare themselves in their countries of origin for their new life. The Oriental Jew came mainly without preparation and without the wish to establish a new society. Many came because they had nothing to lose, and dreamed unrealistic dreams about what would await them in the new country, which they often described as Gan Eden (Paradise). Others came because of their strong bonds with the Jewish tradition and their belief in the Messiah. All of them were quick to discover that the time of the Messiah had not yet come and that life in Israel was difficult and different from what they had expected. Whatever their motivations, they were unprepared for the new conditions. "Shlichim" (emissaries) from Israel had often stimulated these unrealistic and false expectations. In contrast to the average European, the average Oriental is passive. This tends to make adjustment more difficult. Sitting in huts, tents or barracks under primitive and crowded conditions, getting the basic necessities without payment, having unpleasant experiences in human relationships with officials or in contacts at work, in buses, or in the street, were among the negative factors in their absorption. Even where a positive attitude existed toward change and where absorption conditions were positive in material things as well as in human relationships, the breakdown of old patterns and its negative consequences for families could not be avoided.

The Oriental Jew whose family was a patriarchial one, the father being the head and unquestioned authority of the family, found himself suddenly in a democratic society. Not knowing the language, the father had to depend on the child, who was much quicker to learn and to find his way about in the new surroundings. The child, noting the comradeship of Israeli parents and their children, mistook this pattern as freedom from all authority and defied the father, whose word he had never dared question before. He found that he was the one to teach and help his elders. He sensed his parents' inability to help him in adjusting to the new society. Their inability to read or write or to give him anything of the new values were important factors in the breakdown of the family structure and changing roles within the family. The parent, who had seen childhood as a necessary state of evil to be overcome as quickly as possible, who had been asked to marry off his children at the age of 12 or 13, suddenly found himself in a society that prolonged childhood. Not only does this society prohibit child marriage; it values childhood and affords children special privileges. The Oriental father was helpless against society whose demands were so foreign to him. Here he must send his daughters to school instead of marrying them off, and his daughters defy his commands to marry the men he selects. Before, he could punish his daughters; now, he gets punished when he tries to carry out what he considers his right as well as his duty.

New Role for Wife

His wife, who had obeyed him silently, was now the one who often could adapt herself more easily and had less difficulties finding work. Instead of turning her salary over to her husband, she kept it for herself. This, along with her ability to earn, enabled her to take over the house and to push him aside. In the old society, the prevailing pattern had been "Women should not be heard in the presence of men"; in the new society, Israel, women suddenly had the right to vote and to take an equal place beside the men.

The woman who had married a 50-year-old husband when she was 13 suddenly realized when coming to Israel that her husband was old. She also discovered that although she had married him so he would provide for her, she now had to provide for him. He could not find a job, whereas she had no difficulties in getting work as a domestic helper. This change of role brought also a change in the woman's attitude toward her husband. She expressed it not only by defiance of his wishes, but by demands for divorce, by desertion and by complaints to the social worker, police or rabbinical court. Her disrespect toward her husband had, of course, its repercussions in the behavior of the children toward him. And their disobedience toward her was not only an outcome of her outspoken disregard of her husband, but of her inner attitude, which the children were quick to sense.

But her difficulties in rearing the children were to a large extent conditioned by the patterns of child care suddenly imposed on her. Whereas before she gave birth to her children in her own home, she is now expected to go to the hospital. She suddenly finds herself in strange surroundings, being examined by a male physician, an experience shameful and anxiety provoking. She is unable to communicate to those around her who do not understand her language. Her needs and anxieties therefore are not taken care of, as were those of her mother, by women who helped her while giving birth at home. Visiting hours in the hospital are short and sometimes she lives a long way from the hospital, so that none of her family come to see her. It seems reasonable to assume that this early separation of the mother from her child in the hospital may induce a change in attitude toward the newborn. Often women who seem to have adapted themselves very well in the new country express their satisfaction at how lucky they were not to give birth in the new country. Others, not so lucky, try to avoid going to the hospital, preferring the help of relatives and midwives, even though this means losing the government grant paid upon birth of a child.

This anxiety and insecurity are increased as her traditional child-rearing patterns bring her into conflict with government agencies and health centers that help mothers and teach them how to care for their children. The conflicts often arise in the areas of nursing, weaning and toilet training. Other conflicts arise when the child starts going to the kindergarten and to school, since standards of cleanliness and dress often differ. The child that has been shamed by the teacher takes it out on the mother, and this gives rise to a new set of conflicts—conflicts to which the child as well as his parents are inevitably exposed and to which they must adjust in some manner.

This acculturation process is, of course, not unique to the Israeli scene, nor does it have only negative consequences. Many newcomers have adjusted to the new surroundings without evidencing harm. Many have picked up the new without leaving the old life patterns that seem essential and good to them. We stress, however, the negative aspects, since here the problems arise, and here we want to make changes. The index of the negative aspects of acculturation that we have chose to deal with is the great number of requests for child placement on behalf of Oriental Jews.

Behind the Placement

The problem of child placement expresses itself in the following example of a father's demand to have his child placed in a baby home. He himself lives in a hut in a maabarah; there is no running water, the open garbage cans are just outside the house, and flies are everywhere. The child is undernourished, since the father lives on relief. He sees other children playing shashbeck and hanging around instead of learning a trade. If he pushes the child, he might achieve through the child what he himself could not achieve. Consider the words of Mrs. Cohen, from maabarah L. She and her sick husband and 10 children live in a barrack. After her 4-year-old child was returned to her from the toddlers' institution where he was sent for 3 years because of malnutrition and doctor evaluation of mother's "primitiveness in caring for him," she brought him back to the social worker: "Take him. He demands clean sheets and slippers, and I cannot provide this."

The problem expresses itself in the parents' inability to provide for the child who wants the same as the Ashkenazi child. "Here he wants the black the whole day (meaning chocolate ice cream cone); in Yemen there was no such thing." The father's fear of losing his place as the head of the family because his wife has become the wage earner, his wish to run away from the hard reality, together with the apathy he feels because he cannot cope with his problems, often drive him to look for a solution by placing his child. He thus falls in with the existing social climate. He receives without the obligation to give in return, and this increases the demands he makes upon society. "I want my child placed and cared for by the state. It is the state's responsibility." This feeling of dependency brings with it a feeling of hostility that finds its expression in statements like: "When he grows up, Ben-Gurion will take him away to the army anyhow." Behind this approach he hides his frustration in being unable to cope with the new situation, his loss of identity and the sense of belonging, his self-respect. His unexpressed feeling is: "You have taken away everything I had, my house, my place as head of the family. My children do not respect me any longer, take them, they do not belong to me any more anyhow. Before they listened to me, now they listen to the street, the teacher, the youth leader."

We might ask whether the new immigrant's request to place his child means that he is influenced by the social climate in the country, that he has identified with the values of the old-timer, or, on the other hand, reflects the breakdown of his family life, of the bond between parents and child, and therefore represents a negative identification with the values of the absorbing community. Most probably it is a mixture of both.

Workers' Problems

Not only was the community as such unprepared to accept and to understand the newcomers, not only were the newcomers unprepared for what they found in the country of their fathers and the country of their hopes, but those professionals who were to deal with them and help them bridge the old and the new were on the whole entirely unprepared for the problems they had to face.

The professional workers (social workers) were too few to give individual care. They lacked funds and means to provide basic necessities such good housing or nutrition. Many had come to work out of an ideal, and saw their task as changing the newcomer as quickly as possible. Some were members of political parties, and saw their task as not only helping immigrants adjust to the new country, but making converts to their own parties. As these workers themselves had done manual labor, they could not understand the Oriental who preferred to starve rather than do manual work because of the stigma attached to it. Having gone to school herself, the worker fought the father who did not allow his daughter to attend. In retrospect it seems that the worker who had to help the newcomer had perhaps more difficulty understanding the immigrant who had stepped out of another world into the 20th century than vice versa. The worker himself was unable to step out of his frame of reference. Often he took over completely. He, the helper, had to know better and had to have the answer. Bad hygienic conditions, undernourishment, unfamiliarity with the patriarchial family life frightened him. He felt that the burden of responsibility was too great, sometimes leading him to use force where persuasion would not help in dealing with the problems.

The workers, being the givers, often did not make allowances for individual differences. With the giving came the demand or expectation that the receiver would act in accordance with their, the helpers', judgment.

An example of this problem is the following verbatim recording of a Yemenite father trying to explain why his 6-year-old girl does not develop properly.

"The girl was born when we reached H. She was then 1 month old. Sometimes the doctor came and she was in good health. Then he said I want to take the child and he took her by force. They said that she can grow up like in a health center. And we only give the babies the breast and a bit of food. In the hospital they gave her too much food. And the mother said to the nurse: "Don't give her too much food. My children don't eat much." They said to her, "This is not your concern." She said, "The girl is sick from the food." They said: "We will try and don't give her the breast." For 3 weeks we tried. Afterwards the girl did not want to return to the breast. And from the time they took the girl until today there is no spark of life in her. And thanks to the Almighty my other children did not go to the hospital until today, only this girl."

The state of health of the Oriental immigrants, their high infant mortality rate and unhygienic habits, low standards of living and unfamiliarity with Western ideas, as well as their superstitions, gave the basis for the rationalization that they could not be trusted to bring up healthy children. This was stressed even more as many of the parents sent their children to work instead of to school. In addition, because of their own helplessness in the new country, the parents could not be of much help to their children in the task of adjustment.

Although there is at present a reorientation and rethinking with regard to the placement problem, and many social workers recognize the harm placement does, especially to the infant, the fact remains that the Ministry of Welfare has not yet found ways to use its money to keep children at home instead of placing them in institutions.

Self-examination Essential

Every social worker or educator has to look into himself to make sure that he does not carry over his own familial conflicts while dealing with child placement. He must be careful not to take over for the parents, but help the parents be better parents. Because of historical and ideological reasons and problems of absorption of new immigrants mentioned earlier, the social worker or educator has to be even more careful than his colleagues in countries where similar problems do not exist. The social worker or educator must be equipped to face the task of helping the newcomers find a place in the new society. It is important that the worker understand and properly appraise the situation a parent is in when he asks that his child be placed. The worker must try to help him understand why he is making the request and help him find the best solution, which may or may not be child placement. He cannot be influenced too easily by the pressure the parents bring to bear. Though the worker must be aware that the coming to the agency may mean that the parent is still willing to do something for his child, and therefore has to be careful not to negate this readiness by taking too much time in exploring the situation, he must be careful not to take over the parent's responsibility for his child. There are parents who tend to exploit the readiness of the worker to help the child. Much understanding and courage are demanded of the worker not to share society's prejudice against the parents. But he should not get caught in the parents' wish and put the child's development on an entirely material basis by providing him with a hygienic institution.

Only when the worker fully believes and understands that the best place for the child is in his family in most cases, and that everything else is only a substitute, only when he fully believes that the sense of belonging to a family helps to establish healthy ties with society, will he be able to help the child through his parents. Only then will the worker realize that he cannot take over for the parents but has to work with them and to help them to make the best possible plan. He has to help them decide what kind of place is best, to prepare the child and to leave at least some of the financial responsibility to them.

Avoiding Placement

The following example illustrates how and when placement can be avoided. Mrs. B, a 32-year-old widow, mother of four children, came to the agency to apply for placement of the oldest child—a 12-year-old boy. He played truant from school and did not listen to her. In the interviews with the mother, the boy and the teacher, it became clear that the difficulties started after her husband's death 6 months previously. Mrs. B was a newcomer from Yemen and, since she could neither read nor write, was afraid that she could not bring up the boy according to the law. Because of her own upbringing she could not understand her son's wish to play like the Israeli children. She saw her child's behavior as proof of her inability to cope with him. Being afraid of further failure, she asked the worker to take over by placing the boy.

The worker recognized the cultural background of the woman, and saw her capacities to be a mother, which she had proved in many ways. He recognized that by strengthening her and leaving the boy at home, and through tutorial lessons, clubs and work with the mother, she would be able to understand the boy and also her other children as they grew older. Otherwise, they in turn would have to be placed. If the worker had placed the boy, he would not only have deprived the boy of his mother after he had been deprived of his father, but he would have confirmed the mother's feeling that she had failed. Thus, placement in this situation was avoided, and should have been.

Family C was known for years to the agency. The oldest daughter was in an institution, where she had been placed after Mr. C's second marriage 4 years previously because the child was so neglected that the whole neighborhood demanded placement. Since this placement had occurred Mrs. C had given birth to three children. The family was a source of despair to the pediatricians and nurses. The filth in the house was unbelievable. The father did not pay attention to anything in the house; he was harassed making an effort to keep body and soul together. When the fourth child was born, the doctor demanded placement of the newborn, who was undernourished and premature. He insisted on placement because of the "primitiveness" of the mother. He was also against the installation of a stove, which was needed if the baby were to remain at home.

The social worker saw the healthy tie of the mother to the baby. She realized that much of the neglect was due to the mother's inability to find her way in the country, her rather limited intelligence and the objective economic pressure. The worker knew that if the baby were placed, it would be an "orphan" with two living parents, remaining in the institution all her childhood, like many other "short-term" placed children. She also recognized that if Mrs. C did not learn to handle this baby, subsequent children would have to be placed too. Therefore, a plan was worked out in which the doctor, the nurse and a homemaker participated. The allowance to the family was increased. (This was cheaper than placement.) After half a year the baby was the best looking and healthiest one in the community. The house was clean and the mother walked about in a clean housefrock.

But not always can the child remain at home. Death of his wife made Mr. L apply for the placement of his 3- and 7-year-old children. It was obvious that he could not accept his wife's death. He left his house and moved into the overcrowded quarters of his in-laws, who were old and sick and were having a difficult time looking after one retarded son and another emotionally disturbed son. Only when he began to accept what had happened, through the worker's help, was he able to move back to his home, to talk with his son about what had happened and to spend time with his children. He was able later on to agree to placement in a family group home, rather than having his children placed in an institution. He was no longer afraid that the family who kept the group home would take the children away. He helped prepare the children for placement and participated in their upkeep. Thus, by strengthening the father to be a father again, the best possible plan for the children, under the given circumstances, was made.

In a similar case, Mr. B was helped to accept placement of his children in a group home after he saw that the worker did not blame him for his wife's mental illness and did not regard him as a failure, as the relatives of his wife did. The worker sensed the fear of the newcomer, who was familiar with the idea of institutional placement but not with the concept of families' taking care of strange children. Only through the accepting behavior of the worker and by learning from the worker about his parental rights and obligations could the father agree to the placement with a family. He no longer feared that this type of placement meant selling his children. Decisive in helping him make the best plans for the toddlers were his two visits, one with and one without the children, to the family before they were placed.

But not always are we so successful, as the following will illustrate. Mr. D agreed initially to placement of his 5-year-old son in a group home, but later demanded placement in an institution. He projected his own failure to provide for the boy, his wife and the other children upon the group home. He criticized the food, clothing and everything else. In the initial interviews his part in the boy's deviant behavior had never been discussed, nor his tendency to blame everyone but himself for his failure to adjust in the new country. Nobody helped the father to see that part of his wish to have the boy in the institution was his feeling that he had been cheated again. For this reason he felt that the boy had to be placed in a big institution, despite the fact that the child had made a good adjustment to the home.

In contrast to the two former cases, here the failure of successful placement was due to the worker. He did not have the necessary sensitivity and understanding of the problem.

Parent Motivation

In Israel, it is usually the parents who come to ask for placement, and in most instances the mother makes the request. The reasons for the mother's taking the initiative are inherent in cultural, economic and emotional conditions. The mother in most cases carries the main burden of education, and more of the stress of bringing up the children than the father. Most of the social workers are females, and dealing with the agency is mainly a woman's task. The father's going to the agency would mean loss of pay, since in this country most of the agencies are open only during regular working hours. Where the husband deals exclusively with the agency, the reason often is that the agency has become for him a means of making his living and providing for his family. He can thus maintain his self-respect and ensure his place as head of the house without having to go out looking for work.*

The request for placement usually indicates that something has happened to the family life. It may mean marital conflict, economic pressure, illness or death of a member of the family. It may be inability to handle a particular child because of unconscious or conscious rejection, or a special problem such as mental retardation or physical handicap. Sometimes it indicates the parent's wish to escape an unbearable situation or to give up parental responsibility. Many of these parents are immature, difficult to reach, and with a limited capacity for parenthood.

In most cases there is more than one reason behind the request for placement. Parents come after a period of strain, after having tried on their own, with a feeling that they cannot go on anymore. Even though coming to the agency means asking for help, they want the help on their own terms and right away. They resemble the patient who comes to the doctor, gives him the diagnosis of his illness and asks for a certain medicine he has read or heard about from the newspaper or from a neighbor. In many instances parents ask for placement because they have failed their children, and not because the children have failed them. They often deny their failure, projecting it upon the children or upon society. They often place the least-loved child, the troublemaker.

But we see also that in Israel voluntary placement does not carry any social stigma. On the contrary, the request for placement is made easier because of the ideological background. For many, placement itself has the implication of achieving status.

---

* A social phenomenon that deserves further study is the frequent requests for placement voiced by children and adolescents.

In conclusion, Israel's main task has been and for a long time will be that of making one people and one culture out of many people and many cultures. There can be no doubt that the newcomer has to adjust himself to the new country, a process that leaves room for the newcomer to help form and shape the new country. In other words, he cannot be passive, but must have an active part in shaping the new life. To a great extent it will depend on the Yishuv to channel the influence of the newcomers and to turn their drive into positive factors. The situation here is different from that in the United States, where the immigrant found a more stable culture that absorbed him and to which he could adjust. But even in the U.S. he participated to a degree in shaping the society. In Israel the problem of absorption and adjustment of new immigrants becomes almost qualitatively different due to the proportions of immigrants relative to the absorbing group. Not only is there no stable and unified culture, but the number of immigrants is almost equal to that of the absorbing population. This makes the problem of acculturation very complicated, one in which acculturation has to be a reciprocal process. With regard to the problems dealt with here, the request for placement and the avoidance of placement, we have first to try to understand the immigrant and his patterns of behavior so that we can find the ways of helping him with a minimum of destruction and disintegration of his family life.

Our teachers, nurses, social workers, physicians and youth leaders have to get more basic knowledge of cultural variation and become better acquainted with differences in customs and values. We have to put much more emphasis on adult education, so that the gulf between parents and children will not be too great. Not only do we need many more day nurseries and clubs for children and youth, so that they will not have to be placed in institutions because mothers are away at work, and more provision for vocational training, but we need clubs and recreation centers and evening classes for the parents of our children.

We have looked too long at the parents of our children as "the generation of the desert." We have too long taken over for the parents and we have hidden behind the rationalization that mass immigration allows no time for consideration of their problems. We have been too quick to label the different attitudes and values of the newcomers as primitiveness.

Teamwork Needed

The time has come for all those who are interested in child care to sit down and plan together. The professions have to understand more about each other and what each one is doing. The pediatrician and the nurse have to learn that hygiene is not enough and not an end in itself. Perhaps visits to closed institutions of toddlers and infants will help them to get over their disgust and concern with the poor family in the maabarah. Social workers must find means to get the money available for placement in closed institutions and for helping parents to keep their children at home when this is indicated. Social workers have to find ways and means to channel the voluntary organizations in new directions and to take an active part in programs such as those mentioned. Above all, we all have to learn to put more trust in the new immigrant parent and to strengthen him by helping him to help his child, rather than assuming that he is incapable, and taking away his child.

We know that we cannot avoid entirely the disintegration of the changing family and the growing distance between parents and children in a society such as Israel's. We also know that we have to do everything in order to help the child progress through education and training. But we have the obligation to use all our knowledge and all our experience to make this progress as smooth as possible.

Bibliography

English:
Bobly J., Maternal Care and Mental Health. Geneva, 1951.
Burlingham D., and Freud A., Young Children in Wartime; Burlingham D., and Freud A., Infants without Families. London: 1942, 1948.

Hutchinson D.: In Quest of Foster Parents. New York, 1943.
Charnley J., The Art of Child Placement. Minneapolis, 1955.
Eisenstadt S. N., The Absorption of Immigrants. London, 1954.
Frankenstein K. ed., Between Past and Future. Jerusalem, 1954.
Spiro, M. E., "Education in a Communal Village in Israel," Am. Journal of Orthopsychiatry, April, 1955.
Mead M., ed., Cultural Patterns and Technical Changes. UNESCO, 1955.
Kluckhorn C., and Murray H., Personality Formation: The Determinants. Personality in Nature, Society, and Culture. New York, 1953.
Sottong Ph., "The Dilemma of the Parent as Cultural Bearer," Journal of Social Casework, June, 1955.

Hebrew:
Reinhold Ch., Youth Builds Its Home. Jerusalem, 1953.
Rapaport J., "Lebirrur Darcha Shel Alijath Hanoar Wemekoma bechinuch in Israel Megamoth" (Child Welfare Quarterly). Jerusalem, 1953.
Feitelson D., "Education of the Infant and Young Child in the Kurdish Community" (New Immigrants). Megamoth, January, 1954.
"On the Placement of Young Children—A Report." Megamoth, April, 1955.

Staff Consultation in an Israeli Organization for Immigrant Children

This paper constitutes an attempt to illustrate how certain concepts of consultation were used in a children's institution and two collective settlements in Israel. For nearly 2 years the author served as one of several consultants to the child care workers of the Lasker Mental Hygiene Clinic and Youth Aliyah, an organization caring for immigrant children.

The education and professional status of the child care workers varied greatly. Some had been trained as teachers; others had received special training in child care. Their level of skill ranged from professional to semiprofessional.

The Setting

Youth Aliyah is a national organization that during the past 25 years has been responsible for the care of about 80,000 immigrant children, most of whom were between 3 and 17 years of age. Some had been placed with Youth Aliyah by their parents for economic or ideological reasons; many, however, had come to Israel unaccompanied by their

Reprinted with permission of the Family Service Association of America from Social Casework, XLIV, 7, July 1963.

parents. During the 1930s and 1940s the majority emigrated from Europe. In the late 1940s and the 1950s most came from the ghettos of North Africa and Asia. Altogether they came from 72 countries. Often they were the most underprivileged of an underprivileged class.

Youth Aliyah began as an educational movement promoting the ideological tenets of Zionism. Increasingly, it has become a child placement agency—a shift in purpose that the administrators have yet to articulate or fully accept. The organization bears financial responsibility for maintaining the children; their education is conducted in a number of settings with varying degrees of autonomy. Most of the children are placed in so-called normal settings—that is, in a collective farm settlement or a children's institution. Those who are obviously severely damaged are placed in special therapeutic settings.

Over the years the diagnostic procedures employed by Youth Aliyah have improved, but for a variety of reasons many severely disturbed children have still been placed in normal settings. On an average, 400 children are seen in intake each month. Caseworkers and psychologists are in short supply, and many workers lack the knowledge and training needed for an appreciation of the child's individuality, background and cultural patterns. At times a place has had to be found quickly for children suddenly evacuated from dangerous situations. The idealistic founders of Youth Aliyah believed that the experience of living in Israel would in itself heal all wounds; thus, upon his arrival in Israel each child was considered a *tabula rasa* to be educated for the "ideal" collective life in rural areas. Moreover, since it is the philosophy of the country that every Jew has the right to return to Israel, refusal to admit a child is anathema.[1]

In the two kibbutzim from which the following case material was taken, children cared for by Youth Aliyah lived in groups of from 15 to 20. Their ages ranged from 11 to 14. They were housed apart from those whose parents were members of the kibbutz. The youth village had about 500 children, living in groups of 50 to 60. They were divided by age: one division for those between 7 and 13, another for those between 14 and 17.

Since the educational inspector was not in a position to give the child care workers assistance in improving their performance, Youth Aliyah arranged for a social work consultant to provide this service. The consultant was to help the staff handle more appropriately children who were upsetting them or the group. Many of those who were said to show "neurotic symptoms" were in reality reacting to the environment. Almost no casework services were available to them; there was always a waiting list for the limited facilities at the treatment centers.

The relationship between the consultant and the workers was loosely defined. The only powers given to the consultant were arranging for a child to receive a diagnostic work-up at a clinic and recommending his removal to another setting. The workers were free to request consultation services or to avoid them, to come alone or as a group. The workers in each setting also decided on the kind of office space that would be made available to the consultant.

The Nature of Consultation

Consultation is a process of giving and taking help within an interpersonal relationship.[2] Individuals or groups may seek consultation, or it may be thrust upon them by administrative fiat. In either case the value of the service depends upon the consultee's readiness to entertain new ideas and his ability to translate these ideas into skills appropriate to his function and role.[3] A consultative relationship between professional persons may involve a conflict about who is the "expert" in certain areas, since both the consultant and the consultee are accustomed to assuming the role of expert. The use made of consultation depends upon the ability of both parties to clarify and respect the differences in their experience and upon their understanding of the complementary nature of these differences. The consultant's authority rests on his knowledge and expertness. He has no power to recommend promotions, to hire or fire staff; he has no responsibility for the specific work conditions in an organization or for the implementation of his recommendations. In order to establish a relationship with the consultee, he must start where the consultee is. He must be able to assess not only his need for help but also his feelings about taking help. The consultee is not asking for consultation about his personal problems, even though these problems may provide an unconscious motivation for seeking help or may have contributed to creating the specific situation with which he needs help. He may bring to the relationship such emotional needs as dependency, rebelliousness, and fear of authority. The relationship is dynamic, and the consultee's request for help has to be evaluated in terms of how much and how fast it should be given.

A consultant to a group has the added responsibility of keeping the group discussion of a case geared to the capacity of the worker responsible for the actual handling of it.[4] The consultant's work becomes even more complicated when several workers are involved in a case, regardless of whether one or all of them are asking for help. In such situations the consultant has to assess the relationships among the workers and the capacity of each for making use of consultation. Often he must offer them help in working out their relationships.

In such settings as schools and other children's institutions, the consultant needs to understand the manifold relationships between the individuals and the rest of the group and between the individuals and the wider social environment. These relationships must also be viewed within the context of the problems, philosophy and culture of the institution. Although the consultant must be competent in the practice of his profession and must identify himself with its goals, he must also be able to understand the practice and goals of the consultee's profession. With a teacher, for example, the goal is not to change him into a social worker but to help him understand the pupil and thus to increase his knowledge of human motivation and behavior. Through this knowledge and self-understanding, the teacher may find a more fruitful way to work with his pupil.

The consultant's function is to help the consultee discover the truth for himself rather than to uncover it for him. Only when the consultee has the thrill of making discoveries about his work will he be able to integrate and apply them by testing his new knowledge in one case and then transferring it to other situations warranting the same approach.

Establishing a Relationship

In an unstructured, nonauthoritative setting such as the one in which the writer worked, the consultant had to have an attitude of acceptance. Beginning in this way proved to be of great diagnostic value in ascertaining the workers' motivation and readiness to use consultation. It was also useful in understanding the power structure and social relationships in the settings. The consultant started by seeing those persons who came to see her. She had to prove to them that she had something of value to offer them and had to overcome their suspicions of her as a member of a different culture and as a city dweller.

The educational inspector accompanied the consultant on her first visit to Kibbutz X. On the first visit made alone, only one worker was at the kibbutz and she had to hunt for him. He had made no arrangements to provide an office, and only after her arrival did he start looking for space. While he was engaged on this mission he interrupted his progress to transact other business along the way. Finally he chose a bench under a tree. The worker thought that the consultant, like the educational inspector, should visit classes and observe the children's behavior. As on the previous visit, the consultant's way of working and its differences from that of the educational inspector were discussed. Together worker and consultant would look for ways of helping children. The consultant asked the worker how he thought she could be of help. He listened, but seemed not to accept what was said. He did not argue, but began to complain about the previous consultant. The consultant did not explore his obvious resistance to consultation but started with the fact that he was there. She asked about the children, the setting, and the whereabouts of the housemother, who had chosen to show her resistance by absenting herself.

During a discussion of a "bed-wetter," some questions arose that the worker could not answer. Since the housemother could do so, he summoned her to the conference. In this nonthreatening way, he learned the value of her attendance at the conferences and could understand why she should be present. From then on, they participated together in the conferences. It became clear that both the worker and the housemother regarded the former as the person with higher status. The housemother was the more flexible and the more prepared to ask for help. The worker could make only limited use of consultation; his unconscious feeling about consultation did not change much, and he showed resistance and hostility by occasionally forgetting about his scheduled conferences. When an attempt was made to make him conscious of his resistance, he said consultation was an unnecessary addition to his overcrowded schedule.

In Kubbutz Y the situation was different. Here the senior worker received the consultant in his office, which was already prepared for a conference. They were joined by the other three workers on the staff. The senior worker was the most active participant; he did most of the talking and was very controlling. The consultant's goal at Kibbutz Y became not only to hold consultations on the individual child or the group, but to help the senior worker be less controlling and to help the other workers take more responsibility without threatening him or changing the power structure. This goal was achieved slowly and partially. The consultant took the initiative in drawing out the other workers' reactions and made herself available to the senior worker for short, informal discussions.[5] On these occasions they talked about the senior worker's role as an "enabler" to the children and to his co-workers, who were less knowledgeable than he. As a result of recognizing his own importance he stopped talking so much at the consultation conferences. He expressed no open hostility or resistance; consciously, he showed a desire for consultation. On the other hand, he needed to compete and to control, and the other workers accepted his behavior passively. The consultant did not discuss with him, at a deep level, his competitiveness or resistance.

The consultant did deal, however, with the workers' feelings about her own different way of life. They looked upon her as the nonidealist; to the staff the kibbutz represented the highest expression of idealism and the fulfillment of their ideals, and they openly discussed their beliefs. They had been apprehensive that the consultant would turn the children in the direction of the city instead of helping the workers achieve the collectivist ideal. The senior worker feared that the consultant would impose her own set of values and that she might encourage the child to develop his individuality without taking into consideration the need for him to become a member of the kibbutz. After this subject had been discussed, the consultant's relationship with the workers improved considerably.

In the children's village, the consultant was received by the educational director, who discussed the general organization of the village and his view of the function of consultation. He wanted the consultant to remove the disturbed children from the village. They discussed the pros and cons of having him participate in the conferences and the decision was left up to him. He was an experienced educator with a countrywide reputation; even though the consultant wondered whether the workers would feel free to express themselves in his presence, she felt that she had to start where he was. In believing that he had the right to attend, she differed with some of her colleagues, who felt that his authority would not allow the usual relationship between consultant and consultee to develop.

The conferences also illuminated for the consultant the power structure of the children's village. The worker's status in the village was determined by how he handled his job, not by its title. The pattern of resistance observed in the conferences was similar to that encountered at the kibbutzim. Once the consultant's reputation was established, the director of the elementary school, at his own request, started to participate in all the conferences. When a particular problem, such as the work attitude of a child, was discussed, the work instructors joined the group. After a while, the educational director of the older group attended the conference only as the need arose. The educational director of the younger group continued to attend all the conferences, and he helped to facilitate changes in the institution. After the workers overcame their difficulty in expressing themselves in his presence, a better working relationship was established in the group.

In the children's village and in Kibbutz Y, the consultant's goal of developing teamwork was largely achieved. One result of the conferences was that the workers began to meet for preliminary discussion of the case to be presented. This spirit of cooperation found expression in other areas of their work as well. Upon request, the consultant sometimes held individual conferences with the workers. Many of these were "gripe" sessions against colleagues or administrators. Here the focus was to help the worker express his feelings, resentments and questions in front of the group.

The experiences at Kibbutz X, Kibbutz Y, and the children's village illustrate that the consultative relationship is a dynamic, continuous process demanding flexibility and alertness to the power structure. A combination of group and individual conferences is desirable. An unstructured setting permits the consultee to express hostility and resistance without feeling guilty. Although the consultant is permissive and accepting, he has to assume leadership in many situations; when the teamwork is good, he can be more passive.

Focusing on the Child

The primary focus of consultation was on the child and his problems. After the workers had had an opportunity to discuss a number of children and their problems, they began to raise general questions. Thus general concepts regarding intake policy, grouping, and the importance of parents emerged from discussions of problems in specific cases. Another idea that emerged was that the child's physical separation from his parents does not entail emotional separation from them. Also of great importance was the question of the dual loyalty demanded of the child. In certain instances he could not remain true to the values of both his workers and his parents. The parents had placed him with the organization for economic or other reasons of no ideological importance. Youth Aliyah, on the other hand, wanted to educate the child to be a farmer—an occupation often unacceptable to his parents. Caught between opposing value systems, the child found himself thrust into a real cultural conflict.

Most workers had difficulty in accepting the idea that the consultant preferred to talk about the child rather than see him. Workers who have no social work background find it difficult to understand the idea of working with one person to help another. The Youth Aliyah child care workers had difficulty in accepting the idea that their need for help in handling children arose because they did not recognize their own personal problems. They thought the children needed direct help because their own efforts had been unavailing. Asking for help at such a point was an additional complication. They no longer trusted their "objectivity"; suffering from guilt feelings, they asked, "How do you know I am presenting an objective picture of the child?" Less sophisticated workers thought the consultant had some "magic"—that her talking with the child would cure him of his problems. Some workers, of course, were pleased that the consultant did not want to see the child; they feared that the child would "tell on them" or that social workers and psychologists had the power to read minds. They rationalized this fear by saying, "If you see the child, the group will think he is nuts."

Patience and skill were needed for being a consultant to workers who had so many feelings of anxiety, doubt, and distrust. Fortunately, most of the workers had a conscious desire to be helped so that they could help the children. Here was a positive emotion upon which to start building. In spite of pressure from some sophisticated workers, the consultant was careful to avoid professional terms and long, theoretical explanations of dynamics. Questions were answered in simple terms, and an attempt was made to help the workers see the child as an individual. No pretense was made of knowing all the answers. Pointing out that the workers knew more about the child than the consultant could learn in one interview gave them increased confidence in themselves. By encouraging the workers to talk about the child and what they thought was bothering him, the consultant discovered the facts while helping the workers arrive at the diagnosis. The process sometimes took six to eight sessions for one child. Eventually the workers accepted the challenge of the Socratic method. They began to see the child from a new point of view and to find out more about him and his parents. Their self-esteem rose as they uncovered the missing pieces that made a child's behavior understandable. The number of cases that could be dealt with in this way was small in comparison to the total number of children receiving care, but it is to be hoped that the staff will apply the knowledge they acquired in their future work.

Dealing With the Workers' Values

A conflict between the worker and the child may be due to the personality of the worker. Therefore, it was sometimes helpful to compare referrals made by different workers. One referred children who wet the bed; another referred children who stole. The workers in the kibbutz were less tolerant of the thief than of the bed-wetter. By having the workers describe the child, the consultant learned not only the facts, but the workers' feelings. She encouraged them to express their anger toward the child who stole, but also tried to help them understand the possible reasons for his doing so. An "open" community was too much of a temptation for some children. Compared with the settled residents of the kibbutzim, many of the Youth Aliyah children and their parents might be considered "have-nots." By being nonjudgmental and refusing to condemn them or hold them responsible for the child's stealing, as their superegos and others in the kibbutz did, the consultant released the workers' anger and frustration and freed them to look at the child less emotionally.

At other times the workers were helped to see that the reason so little was known about a child was not that he was withdrawn but that no one had taken the trouble to ask him about himself. Once a worker started making inquiries, the child began to talk and no longer seemed shut up within himself. Consultation helped the workers recognize that many of the children had come from cultures in which there was little reverence for learning. Therefore, they had received little stimulation, and a desire to achieve had to be instilled in them. In other words, by discovering the significance of differing cultural values, the workers became more attuned to what the children were like. They also began to see that the consultant was not attacking their values but rather helping them to understand that these children were caught between two competing value systems.

Through consultation the workers were helped with a number of other problems. Some workers had to learn to accept the child's parents rather than lower their prestige in the child's eyes, which would only increase the child's struggle against the workers' values. Another difficulty was the workers' attitude that parents, "the generation of the desert," were not important; the children represented the future, and devoted workers could bring about their transformation. One can speculate on the extent to which the workers' revolt against their own parents was a factor in their having these attitudes. Rather than explore the workers' attitudes, motivations, or relationships with their parents, the consultant continued to focus on the child, trying to present him as a human being in his own right. The workers were asked to find answers to the questions, Who are the child's parents? Does he write to them? Do they write to him? Does he ask for vacations? Differences in motivation between the workers and the children were discussed without threatening the workers' defenses. They sought to live in a collective settlement because they were idealistic; the children, however, came to the kibbutz or youth village because they were sent there by their parents.

Sometimes the consultant found it necessary to give direct advice; it was not always possible to sit back and ask, "What do you think?" The direct approach, however, had to be used carefully and with good judgment. Sometimes the consultant suggested leading questions the workers could ask a child: "How did you come here? Did your brother come too?" Gradually, the workers' attitudes changed, and it was gratifying to see them making home visits and inviting the parents to visit them. The workers themselves were then able to recognize the importance of parents for the child.

Sometimes the consultant had to "soft-pedal" the workers' enthusiasm about the astonishing progress they reported some youngsters were making. Even when a given child had indeed ceased to be a problem, as happened in a number of instances, this improvement was not always permanent.

In time, the consultant came to question the advisability of her original plan of not interviewing children. She decided that seeing a child might enable her not only to become acquainted with him but also to understand his impact on the worker through feeling his impact on herself. Therefore, she began to interview some of the children. Sometimes she, too, was unable to "get the child to talk" and was just as puzzled about the diagnosis as the worker was. Her admission of her failures helped relieve the workers of their feelings of inadequacy.[6] Moreover, the workers were not competent to evaluate deeply disturbed children. By interviewing these children directly, the consultant was able to spot more quickly those who needed direct treatment in a special institution or in a mental hospital.

The danger, however, in the consultant's interviewing the child was that she might take over the worker's role instead of adding to his understanding. Some workers were so insecure that, to help them over a crisis, it was preferable for the consultant to interview the child and report back to them. Occasionally the children themselves asked to see the consultant. When the workers became more comfortable with her, she became known as the worker of the workers. She also attended most of the important celebrations in the collectives. Her attendance was important to the workers, because they felt that they and the children appeared at their best on such occasions.

Interplay and Dynamics in the Group Session

Communication among workers is a most important aspect of work in a children's institution. Through group discussion the worker learns how he himself views the child and what his coworkers think and feel. He learns new aspects of the child's life. He gains the experience of reaching an agreement with other members of the staff on the handling of a child. He realizes that there is room for different opinions about the handling of children. He can let off steam. Through these interchanges he may decide to revise his techniques or he may become more comfortable in using them. His respect for other staff members' functions increases. He may find comfort when he realizes that everyone has difficulty in handling certain children. When he is able to see progress in at least one area, his hope is strengthened.

The consultant must be aware of the interaction in the group and must prevent the members from directing their hostility against one another. He must curb the worker who talks too much and exposes too many of his feelings or personal problems. The group may unite against the consultant and try to force his consent to the removal of a child, thus indirectly venting their anger and frustrations and indicating that they really do not feel the consultant is helpful.

The consultant sometimes helped the group members express their resistance openly, but she believed that better results were achieved and less anxiety produced if the discussions remained child-centered instead of worker-centered. Her primary function was to help the child rather than to help the workers resolve their personal difficulties. The purpose of consultation was not to provide therapeutic sessions for the workers, but to change their attitudes toward the child by increasing their understanding of him.

Conclusions and Implications

In this article, certain additional tools of consultation—such as campuswide meetings and lectures—have not been discussed. Moreover, important contacts with the educational supervisors and administrators of Youth Aliyah and the child-care settings have not been described. It should be pointed out, however, that most of the direct work with the workers would have been wasted without administrative support. Consultation alone can do little to improve the environment and help workers who are providing direct service use themselves to their fullest capacity.

Casework consultation makes an important contribution as a corrective and preventive method in the field of mental health. But it is not an adequate substitute for direct casework with children who suffer from severe neurotic disturbances or primary behavior disorders. Either such children must be placed in a psychiatric setting or, if they are to remain in the institution, casework service must be made available to them and consultation be made available to their educators.

When the consultant accepts the consultees' resistance and focuses on the case, they realize they can make use of consultation without feeling threatened. The combination of individual and group conferences and of formal and informal meetings adds to the workers' understanding of casework and helps them function as a team.

The process of consultation has a reeducative element that extends beyond the provision of individual guidance; it also fulfills a teaching function. The consultant helps the workers and the child care institution as a whole to integrate into their approach basic social work concepts such as the individualization of the child.

References

1. Joseph Neipris and Jona Rosenfeld, "The Educational Group—Problems," *Alim*, January 1951 (Jerusalem, Hebrew); Moshe Kol, Youth Aliyah: Past, Present and Future, International Federation of Children's Communities (UNESCO publication), Jerusalem, 1957; Leon Uris, Exodus, Doubleday and Co., Garden City, New York, 1958; Melford Spiro, Kibbutz: Venture in Utopia, Harvard University Press, Cambridge, Massachusetts, 1956; Jona Rosenfeld and Gerald Caplan, "Techniques of Staff Consultation in an Immigrant Children's Organization in Israel," *American Journal of Orthopsychiatry*, Vol. XXIV, January 1954, pp. 42-58.

2. Doris Siegel, "The Function of Consultation: Some Guiding Principles for Medical Social Workers," in Symposium Proceedings, 1953, Graduate School of Social Work, University of Pittsburgh, Pittsburgh, Pennsylvania, 1953.
3. Mildred Sikkema, "The School Social Worker Serves as Consultant," in Casework Papers, 1955, presented at the Eighty-second Annual Forum of the National Conference of Social Work, San Francisco, California, May 29-June 1, 1955, Family Service Association of America, New York, 1955, p. 77.
4. Ralph Ormsby, "Group Psychiatric Consultation in a Family Casework Agency," Social Casework, Vol. XXXI, November 1950, p. 362.
5. See Beulah Parker, Psychiatric Consultation for Nonpsychiatric Professional Workers, Public Health Monograph No. 53, U.S. Public Health Service, Department of Health, Education, and Welfare, Government Printing Office, Washington, D.C., 1958, p. 3.
6. See Mary Jean Riley, "Psychiatric Consultation in Residential Treatment. Workshop, 1957. 4. The Child Care Worker's View," American Journal of Orthopsychiatry, Vol. XXVIII, April 1958, pp. 283-88.
7. Marvin Adland, "Psychiatric Consultation in Residential Treatment. Workshop, 1957. 5. Discussion," American Journal of Orthopsychiatry, Vol. XXVIII, April 1958, pp. 289-90.

DATE DUE